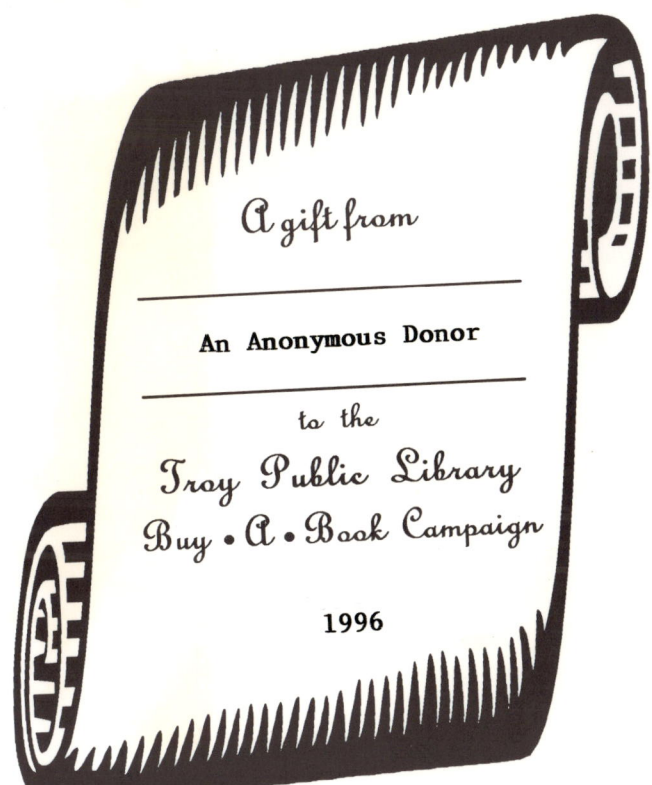

A gift from

An Anonymous Donor

to the
Troy Public Library
Buy • A • Book Campaign

1996

HEMEROCALLIS
Day Lilies

HEMEROCALLIS
Day Lilies

Walter Erhardt

*translated from the German by Alexander Helm
edited by Diana Grenfell*

KANGAROO PRESS

© B.T. Batsford Ltd, 1992

(A translation of *Hemerocallis Taglilien [Hemerocallis Day Lilies]* by Walter Erhardt © Verlag Eugen Ulmer, Stuttgart, 1988)

Drawings by Marlene Gemke

All rights reserved. No part of this publication may be reproduced, in any form or by any means, without permission from the Publisher

Typeset by Best-set Typesetter Ltd, Hong Kong
and printed in Great Britain by Bookcraft, Midsomer Norton

This translation published by
Kangaroo Press Pty Ltd
3 Whitehall Road (P.O. Box 75)
Kenthurst NSW 2156

ISBN 0 86417 451 9

CONTENTS

List of Colour Plates	7
List of Line Illustrations	9
Picture Acknowledgements	11
Foreword	13

History of the Day Lily
- Chinese Tradition — 15
- Before Linnaeus — 17
- The Plant Hunters — 20
- Stout and the History of the American Hemerocallis Society — 21
- Europe in the Twentieth Century — 22
- Trends in Recent Years — 26

The Species
- Place in the Plant Kingdom — 28
- Physical Characteristics — 29
- Classification — 31
- Identification Key to the Species — 32
- Description of the Species — 35

Modern Hybrids
- Colours and patterns — 60
- Flower Shapes — 65
- Flowering Habits — 68
- Growth Habits and Leaf Forms — 69
- Diploid and Tetraploid Types — 71

Making the Choice
- Factors to Consider — 73
- Yellow is not just Yellow — 74
- Red Varieties for cold Climates — 80
- Pink and Related Tones — 83
- Near-white and Blue-toned varieties — 87
- Patterns for Enhancement — 91
- American Hemerocallis Society Awards — 94

Propagation and Selection of Hybrids
- Pollination and Fertilisation — 98
- Special Breeding Projects — 102
- Cultivation and Selection of Plants — 105
- Selection and Registration — 107
- *Hemerocallis* raised in Europe — 109
- German Awards — 112

CONTENTS

Vegetative Propagation
  Dividing the Root   113
  Dividing the Crown   114
  Proliferations   115
  The Lanoline-BAP-IAA
    Method   116
  Tissue Culture   118

Cultivation of Day Lilies
  Obtaining Plants   120
  Planting   120
  Siting   122
  Watering and Mulching   123
  Fertilisers and General Care   125
  Diseases and Pests   126

Making the Most of Day Lilies
  In the Garden   130

  Companion Plants   133
  Day Lilies in Floral Art   135
  Photographing Day Lilies   136
  Day Lilies on the Menu   140

Appendices
  I *Societies*   143
  II **Hemerocallis** *Sources*   144
  III *First Descriptions of*
    Hemerocallis *Species*   146
  IV *Excluded Names*   148

Bibliography   149
General Index   152
Index of Species, Varieties
  and hybrids   156

COLOUR PLATES

Day lilies are not only suitable for borders, as shown here, but some are also suitable for lightly wooded areas, rose beds, edging ponds, binding sloping sites, landscaping civic and municipal areas and public parks.

Hemerocallis species
top left: *Hemerocallis exaltata*
top right: *H. dumortieri*
centre left: *H. forrestii* 'Perry's Variety'
centre right: *H. lilioasphodelus*
bottom left: *H. fulva* 'Europa'
bottom right: *H. fulva* 'Kwanzo'

Yellow *Hemerocallis* varieties
top left: 'Sunstar' (Lester, 1954 USA)
top right: 'Golden Chimes' (Fischer, 1954 USA)
centre left: 'Green Puff' (Spalding, 1977 USA)
centre right: 'Double Glitter' (Krupien, 1976 USA)
bottom left: 'Double Glitter' (Krupien, 1976 USA)
bottom right: 'Osage Delight' (McKeithan, 1954 USA)

Red *Hemerocallis* varieties
top left: 'Christmas Carol' (Wild, 1971 USA)
top right: 'Red Roque' (McKinney, 1977 USA)
centre left: 'Margaret Marlatt' (Lambert, 1968 USA)
centre right: 'Spanish Brocade' (Allgood, 1973 USA)
bottom left: 'Bess Ross' (Claar, 1951 USA)
bottom right: 'Willie Bill' (Williamson, 1971 USA)

Pink *Hemerocallis* varieties
top left: 'Frank Gladney' (Durio, 1979 USA)
top right: 'Mini Skirt' (Lambert, 1966 USA)
centre left: 'Sari' (Munson, 1983 USA)
centre right: 'Cleo Barnwell' (Stutson, 1972 USA)
bottom left: 'Lullaby Baby' (Spalding, 1975 USA)
bottom right: 'Fairy Tale Pink' (Pierce, 1980 USA)

Blue and white *Hemerocallis* varieties
top left: 'Jade Star' (Moldovan, 1978 USA)
top right: 'Chicago Knobby' (Marsh, 1974 USA)
centre left: 'Catherine Woodbery' (Childs, 1967 USA)
centre right: 'Forget Me Not' (Brown-Lankart, 1971 USA)
bottom left: 'Shinto Shrine' (Moldovan, 1975 USA)

COLOUR PLATES

bottom right: 'Serene Madonna' (Childs, 1972 USA)

Hemerocallis hybrids from central Europe
top left: 'Berlin Premiere' (Tamberg, 1979 FRG)
top right: 'Vienna Butterfly' (Zelina, Austria, not registered)
centre left: 'Berlin Eyed' (Tamberg, FRG, not registered)
bottom left: 'Cologne Morning Glow' (Stobberg, FRG, not registered)

bottom right: 'Pfennigparade' (Köhlein, 1981, FRG)

top: *Hemerocallis* selection. In the grounds of the Palm Garden in Frankfurt day lilies have been planted extensively. There is also a special section for central European and miniature varieties. The two detail pictures show examples of miniature varieties.
bottom left: 'Siloam Bo Peep' (Henry, 1978 USA)
bottom right: 'Little Women' (Wild, 1969 USA)

LINE ILLUSTRATIONS

1 First illustration of a day lily, dating back to the Sung dynasty *16*
2 The Emerocallis of Dioscorides *17*
3 The first European illustrations of *Hemerocallis* *18*
4 Morphology of *Hemerocallis* *30*
5 Growth habits and comparative sizes of *Hemerocallis* species (1) *34*
6 *Hemerocallis altissima* *36*
7 *Hemerocallis aurtantiaca* *37*
8 *Hemerocallis citrina* *38*
9 *Hemerocallis coreana* *39*
10 *Hemerocallis darrowiana* *40*
11 *Hemerocallis dumortieri* *41*
12 *Hemerocallis esculenta* *42*
13 *Hemerocallis exaltata* *42*
14 *Hemerocallis forrestii* *43*
15 *Hemerocallis fulva* *44*
16 Growth habits and comparative sizes of *Hemerocallis* species (2) *46*
17 *Hemerocallis fulva* var. *littorea* *48*
18 *Hemerocallis graminea* *50*
19 Growth habits and comparative sizes of *Hemerocallis* species (3) *51*
20 *Hemerocallis lilioasphodelus* *52*
21 *Hemerocallis* × *luteola* *53*
22 *Hemerocallis middendorffii* *53*
23 *Hemerocallis minor* *54*
24 *Hemerocallis multiflora* *55*
25 *Hemerocallis nana* *56*
26 *Hemerocallis plicata* *57*
27 *Hemerocallis thunbergii* *57*
28 Colour patterning of *Hemerocallis* flowers *62*
29 Additional designs result from the colour of the median stripe, the throat and the tips of the segments *64*
30 The shapes of *Hemerocallis* flowers *66*
31 Pollination *99*
32 Abscission *107*
33 After separation the foliage should be trimmed into a fan shape *114*
34 A cross-section of the crown can succeed only if the attached root system is well developed *115*
35 Proliferations should be pushed into the soil together with that portion of the scape to which they are attached *116*
36 A few weeks after the crown has been cut and treated, new shoots will sprout from it *116*
37 When planting, spread the roots around the heap of soil in the bottom of the hole *121*
38 Damage caused by the three main *Hemerocallis* pests *128*
39 Simplicity is the essence of this day lily arrangement *135*
40 A combination of day lilies and summer flowers makes a beautiful arrangement *136*

PICTURE ACKNOWLEDGEMENTS

All the photographs for the colour plates and the title picture are by the author, except the first, which is by F. Köhlein; and the following opposite page 64: 'Frank Gladney', 'Sari', 'Fairy Tale Pink', and 'Lullaby Baby', all of which are by Roger Grounds.

The line diagrams are by Marlene Gemke, based on suggestions by the author and on reference books.

FOREWORD

At the end of the second world war only a few enthusiasts in Europe were familiar with the *Hemerocallis* genus; and it was not until ten years ago that this sorry state of affairs began to change. The day lily has been one of the most popular garden plants in the United States for many years, and gradually its magnificent appearance is gaining recognition in Europe too. The American Hemerocallis Society (AHS) is rightly proud of its place as one of the largest societies for plant-lovers in the world and is constantly welcoming new members.

What are the reasons for this popularity? Above all, day lilies are beautiful, but of course so are many other plants. The day lily has other advantages: it is easy to care for and not overly susceptible to disease and pests. Moreover, there is a different sort for every style of garden. Plants range in height from 20 to 150cm and the flower size can be as small as 5cm or as large as 20cm. There is a huge variety of colours and flower patterns. Far from causing gardeners a lot of work, the plants actually make life easy for them. The foliage deprives weeds of light and, because day lilies attract so few diseases and pests, toxic chemicals are not required. However, despite all these points in its favour, the day lily has only recently become well-known in Europe.

In view of the above I am indebted to my publishers for allowing me to put together such a detailed look at this plant, introducing it to a broad readership in this splendidly-designed book. I would like to thank the following for their assistance during the preparation of this book: Agnes Bartunek (editing), Dieter Kleinschrot (design) and Marlene Gemke (illustrations). Without the international support I received, my task would have been impossible, and I would like to thank the following for supplying me with a huge variety of specialist information: Mr and Mrs Rieck (FRG), François Verhaert (Belgium), Dick Kitchingman (UK), John Schabell (USA) and Dr Thomas Barr (USA). I must also express my gratitude to Prof Karl Zimmer (Hanover), who as specialist consultant made numerous invaluable contributions.

Above all I would like to thank Fritz Köhlein, who has supported me

FOREWORD

throughout the past few years and become a very valued friend of the family in the process. Last but not least, my thanks go to my wife, for her assistance with the preparation of the book, and in particular for her hard work in the garden – without her support our stock of over 500 types of day lily would never have materialised.

Walter Erhardt

THE HISTORY OF THE DAY LILY

Chinese Tradition

In the West day lilies are grown purely as ornamental plants, but in China, where they have been cultivated for thousands of years, they are grown for other reasons too. They are grown as food plants, as well as for their medicinal value. Their blooms and their flower buds are tasty and nutritious, and their roots and crowns are used in medicine. They also feature as motifs in both poetry and paintings.

Day lilies are mentioned in one of the earliest known collections of Chinese folk songs, the 'Shi-ching', which is said to date back to Confucius (551–479 BC). In the section called 'Wei-feng' there is a poem about the ancient province of Wei that reads:

> O my brother you must go hence
> As warrior of our monarch.
> Steadfastly protect the crown.
> As the day lily (*Hsüan Ts'ao*)
> Behind yon tree,
> Protect me 'gainst misery.

The province of Wei, which flourished during the Chou Dynasty (1122–255 BC), was in northern China. The day lily, which grows there to this day, is *Hemerocallis lilioasphodelus*. Its Chinese name, 'Hsuan', signifies 'to forget', while the word 'Ts'ao' means a bush, so that in Chinese the day lily is known as the 'forgetting plant'. More will be said later of the putative ability of young shoots to heighten awareness and cause hallucinations.

The first book on day lilies was written in 304 BC by Chi Han, the Prefect of Hsing Yang. His small book was entitled *An Introduction to Day Lilies*. Hsing Yang corresponds roughly with the present-day province of Hu-peh, which is where several day lily species grow wild. Han records that his local day lily was called Lu Tsung and differed from the day lily mentioned in the poem, the 'forgetting plant', since its flowers were striped and spotted, but in fact this was not the case. The differences were due solely to differing soil conditions: in poor soil, flower colouring is clearer and purer.

Regardless of whether or not these two species are the same, they grow in many parts of China. Records from eastern China show that as well as *H.*

lilioasphodelus, *H. citrina*, *H. multiflora*, *H. altissima* and *H. fulva* var. *rosea* were also well known. The earliest illustrations of day lilies are to be found in *Materia Medica* from the Sung Dynasty, 1059 AD.

However, almost 500 years earlier Li Shih-chen wrote a medical work entitled *Pen Ts'ao Kang Mu*, in which he writes: 'Day lilies like moist situations. Although new leaves replace the old, the plant remains green almost throughout the whole year. The stems appear in June. The flowers have six petals and four appendages.'* 'They open in the morning and close in the evening. The plant continues blooming into late autumn. There are three kinds, red, yellow and purple.' He then comments upon the names other botanists had given *Hemerocallis*. These are Lu Tsung, Wang Yu, Tan Chi and Liao Ch'ou. 'Lu Tsung' means something like 'stag bulb' and Li Shih-chen mentions that day lilies can be used as an antidote to poisons. 'Wang Yu', on the other hand, means 'dispeller of woe' and this suggests its use as an antidepressant.

Li also records that day lilies had other medicinal uses. A drink made from pounding the roots and soaking them in alcohol was believed to help cure breast abcesses. The remaining pulp was applied externally as a poultice. A quarter-ounce of dried and ground root mixed with rice and taken before each meal was thought to cure dropsy. A tea prepared from the boiled roots acted as a diuretic and was supposed to help in cases of anuria, a disease that may eventually lead to death through uraemia. For intestinal bleeding a mixture of gin, day lily root and roasted ginger was taken. Finally, the juice of the root has proved to be an effective antidote in cases of arsenic poisoning.

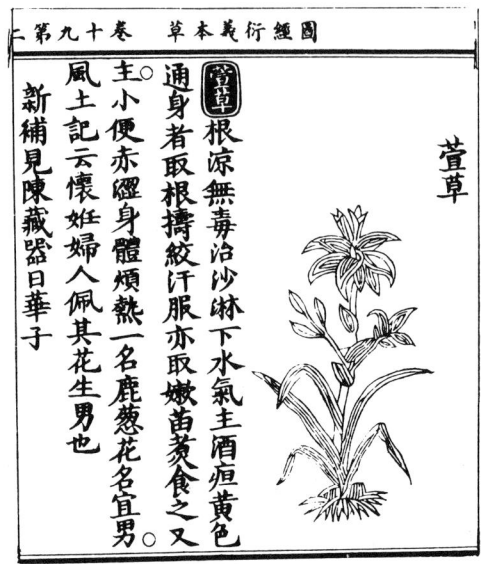

Figure 1 First illustration of a day lily dating back to the Sung Dynasty (1059 BC).

The son of the first emperor of the Ming dynasty had a garden that contained more than 400 sorts of edible plants. In his book, which appeared in 1409 AD, he mentions *Hemerocallis*. Pao Shan, a Buddhist monk, gives the following account of how day lilies should be prepared for the table in his treatise *On the Intensive Production Of Edible Wild Plants*: 'The young shoots are steeped in hot water until they are saturated; then washed, dried and prepared with salt and sesame oil.' Such blanching probably gets rid of undesirable hallucigens.

Day lilies were also widely grown simply as garden flowers. In *Flower*

---

* Presumably Li had overlooked two filaments.

Mirror ('Hua Ching'), which was published in 1688 AD, Chen Hao-Tsu wrote that there were three types of day lily. He mentions a yellow sort with a reddish tinge, as well as a similar one, which was a double. The third kind had smaller, honey-coloured flowers that were scented. 'People with large gardens,' he wrote, 'should plant an abundance of day lilies. In spring the young shoots can be eaten as a vegetable. In summer the blooms also make a nutritious addition to the diet.* One should not, however, eat any part of the double variety since it contains a lethal poison!' In Chen's lifetime his own garden was known as 'the Paradise on Earth'.

To this day in some parts of Asia, the dried foliage, which is quite tough, is plaited into cord, and then used for making footwear. There are few plants that are so versatile that they can be grown for so many diverse purposes.

Before Linnaeus

In 1937 G.P. Baker stated, in *The Journal of the Royal Horticultural Society* that the genus *Hemerocallis* had been known to the Greeks some two thousand years before, but this was probably due to a misreading of the Greek, for although Dioscorides, the ancient Greek natural philosopher, described a plant called *Emerocallis* in his *De Materia Medica*, it was, as the accompanying illustration clearly

Figure 2 The *Emerocallis* of Dioscorides (512 AD) is not a day lily.

shows, an onion. The great Linnaeus adapted this name when he created the genus *Hemerocallis*, although the same name and spelling had been used by the Italian botanist Pierandrea Mattiola (1500–77) in his commentaries on Dioscorides. He probably meant the Mediterranean lily, but one needs to exercise some care since day lilies were only introduced into Europe in the sixteenth century.

The first true references to *Hemerocallis* as we know the genus today, were either by Rembert Dodoens (Dodonaeus, 1517–87), or Charles di Ecluse (Clusius, 1526–1609) or Mathias de Lobel (Lobelius, 1538–1616), though it is now impossible to say which, for all three were close friends and shared their knowledge freely with each other. Indeed, they even collaborated to the extent of allowing illustrations from their books to be used by each other.

---

* In Chinese cookery *H. esculenta* is used as a vegetable either fresh or dried. 'Gum tsoy' (= golden vegetable) or 'gum jum' (= golden needles) are often added to soups or noodles.

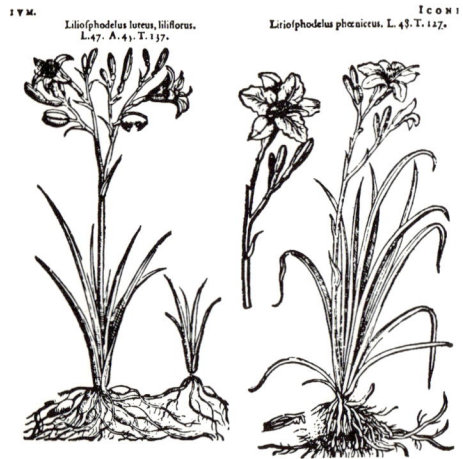

Figure 3 The first European illustrations of *Hemerocallis* published in 1576; left: by Dodonaeus; right: by Lobelius.

One of the earliest references can be found in Pena and Lobel's *Stirpium adversaria nova* (1570). It states: '*Liriosphodelus* blooms in great profusion in the wild, and the old is as beautiful as the young. We saw excellent examples in Venice and Antwerp. The roots are white, like those of the asphodel, but thinner. The stems are about 70cm long. The leaves come directly from the roots and resemble those of the leek, but are more tender. The stalk branches at the end; each of these branches carries three or four yellow or orange lily flowers. These are succeeded by oval-shaped seed capsules that contain the black ovoid seeds, looking rather like those of the paeony. In the "Pharmacopoeia" of Venice the plant is called *Lilium luteum* or *Asphodelum*.'

It is important to realise that what Pena and Lobel were describing is the 'Yellow Day Lily', of which they saw examples in Venice and Antwerp. They took care to provide accurate data as to height, branching and colour, and they were the first to use the name *Liriosphodelus*. It is a pity that they did not include an illustration of the plant. This was rectified when Lobel published *Plantarum seu Stirpum Historia* in 1576. Although the second volume of this new two-volume work is simply a reprint of the original publication, there is on page 47 of the first volume a beautiful woodcut of *H. lilioasphodelus* under the title *Lilioasphodelus luteus liliflorus*.

One page further on there is an illustration and description of *Liriosphodelus phoeniceus*, which we now call *Hemerocallis fulva*. It was described as follows: 'This type has yellowish-red blooms. Its leaves are broader and stronger than those of *Liriosphodelus*. Each plant has two or three round stalks about 45cm or more in length. In addition there are striped lily flowers, which more or less resemble the small Punic lily. The roots are tube-like and smaller than those of the yellow asphodel...' On the basis of these two descriptions and the illustrations, we can now be certain that up until 1576 two kinds of day lily had been introduced to Europe. Since both Venice and Antwerp are sea ports, it may be assumed that the plants came to Europe over the seas.

The next book in which day lilies are mentioned is Clusius' work about the plants of Austria and Hungary. Clusius was an extraordinary man and led an adventurous life until he eventually accepted a professorship at the University of Leyden. He travelled the world in pursuit of his botanical studies and during 1579 and 1580 he was the guest of Baron

Balthasar de Batthyany, residing in the latter's castle in Hungary. There he found innumerable examples of *H. lilioasphodelus*. After he had taken some of these with him to Austria, he was able, twenty years later, to write proudly in his *Rariorum Plantarum Historia* that as a result of his introduction they were now growing everywhere in the gardens of Austria and Germany. Although botanists would later suggest that the species grew wild in Europe, we can be sure that these had in fact, originated from cultivated stock.

In 1554, before either of his friends, Dodoens, who also taught at Leyden, published an illustration of *H. lilioasphodelus*, although he calls it *Lilium luteum*. In his *Cruydeboek* the description is similar to that given by Lobel, but the following additional remark is of interest: 'The yellow lily is, for the time being, known as *Lilium luteum*. At present no other name is known. However, some would call it *Hemerocallis*, which is the Greek description of a flower which opens in the morning when the sun rises and closes again in the evening.' It is interesting to note that as long ago as 1554 the name *Hemerocallis* was mooted, but it would be another 200 years before this name was finally established by Linnaeus.

During the next 200 years nothing changed very much. New books merely reiterated information about the same two species; no new kinds were added. There are illustrations of these two in *Eicones Plantarum* (1590) by Jakob Theodor (who was better known as Tabernaemontanus). He calls the two sorts *Asphodelus liliaceus luteus* and *rubens*. A *Niewe Herball* of 1557 is the famous English translation by Henry Lytes of the book by Clusius, and in this the picture of *H. lilioasphodelus* is labelled *Lilium non bulbosum*. It is not until Gerard's *Herball*, published 40 years later, that we meet for the first time the term 'day lily'.

John Parkinson in *Paradisi in Sole Paradisus Terrestris* of 1629 merely uses copies of Lobel's woodcuts. In 1680, however, Morison suddenly gives us three species of day lily: *Luteus major*, *Luteus minor* and *Puniceus* (or *Phoenicus*). *L. minor* and *L. major* were both yellow-flowered, though we are still not certain to which sort the term *L. major* refers. In 1688, John Ray published his monumental *Historia Plantarum*, which was a compendium of all works previously published in England, and it seems that by then the terms 'day lily' and 'red day lily' were in common usage.

The binomial system of nomenclature was introduced by Carl von Linné (Linnaeus) in 1753 in his *Species Plantarum*. How he deals with *Hemerocallis* is discussed in the chapter entitled 'The Species'. Suffice it to say here that the two editions of *Species Plantarum* (1753 and 1762) differ. In the earlier edition Linnaeus took the view that there was only the one sort of *Hemerocallis*, namely *H. lilioasphodelus*, of which there were two forms, *alpha flavus* and *beta fulvus*. Nine years later he dropped the name *lilioasphodelus* and replaced it with two separate species, *H. flava* and *H. fulva*.

The Plant Hunters

The 200 years that followed Linnaeus are of much greater interest in terms of new day lily species. Indeed, it was during this period that most of the other species were discovered. It was the great era in which men set out to explore, map and measure the world and as a rule the expeditions included not only geographers and geologists but also botanists. Some people even set out on their own, with the sole intention of discovering new plants and bringing them back to Europe.

The next species to make its début in Europe, still before the end of the eighteenth century, was *H. minor*. It was described by Miller in his *Gardener's Dictionary* of 1768. Miller was the head gardener at the Chelsea Physic Garden in London, and the dictionary was a descriptive catalogue of the plants growing there and their cultural needs. At much the same time Carl Peter Thunberg, who had studied under Linnaeus and collected plants in Japan between 1775 and 1776, recorded in his *Flora Japonica* that several varieties of *H. fulva* existed apart from the normal sort. He mentions one with double flowers, as well as one with variegated leaves.

It was not until the nineteenth century that the search really gathered momentum. All across Europe changes in tax laws meant that glass was suddenly cheap and plentiful and those who could afford it built conservatories, which were often quite vast. This in turn led to an enormous demand for plants to grow in these conservatories. Plant hunters searched far and wide to satisfy this demand, but it was also a period when the search for scientific knowledge was gaining ground. German and Austrian experts were, for example, studying sterility in *H. fulva*.

In 1802 a botanical artist named Andrews published an illustration of the grass-leafed day lily *H. graminea*. This species had probably been available in Europe for some time, although nothing is known about how it arrived. Equally *H. fulva* var. *disticha* must have been known in Britain before 1804, even though it was not until 1812 that Sims, in an article in *Curtis' Botanical Magazine*, mentioned a picture of it that was in the possession of Sir Joseph Banks; this was by a Chinese artist and was dated 1793. This day lily did not flower in Britain until 1823. It came, as did so many plants in the early nineteenth century, from southern China.

Macao and Canton were important trading posts at this period and Jesuit missionaries were proselytising in Peking. It was from these areas that the first Chinese plants to reach Europe came. Not only did Europeans send plants home, but the Chinese themselves were highly enterprising. Their despatches from Hua-ti (the Land of Flowers) soon furnished their clients in the West with quantities of popular garden plants, chrysanthemums, camellias, paeonies and later roses and rhododendrons. Only the day lily lagged behind, perhaps because it was more difficult to ship.

Gradually, however, the day lilies arrived, first the double-orange *H. fulva* 'Flore Pleno' (1869) and later the lemon-yellow *H. citrina* and *H. fulva* var. *maculata*. These last two arrived in Italy, where Charles Sprenger and Willy Müller were instrumental in the introduction of new plant species. *H. middendorffii*, which comes from Siberia, arrived soon after and *H. dumortieri* came from Japan. Time and again species arrived whose origins still cannot be explained. Among these are the brilliant orange *H. aurantiaca* and the lovely, scented, pale yellow *H. thunbergii*. Despite these new species, however, until the year 1900 only about half the known species had been introduced into Europe or America.

Stout and the History of the American Hemerocallis Society

At about the turn of the century a new era for day lilies began. This was largely due to the efforts of botanist, scholar, plant breeder and day lily enthusiast, Dr Arlow B. Stout. He wrote numerous articles about day lilies and his book *Day Lilies*, published in 1934, is still the standard work; it was re-issued in an updated edition in 1986.

Stout's great achievement was firstly his classification of the species of day lilies based on a thorough morphological investigation and, secondly, his breeding programe, which paved the way for future breeders. Even though his classification has needed some subsequent revision, his investigations into the genetics of the genus *Hemerocallis* established the fundamental relationships of the species. His hybrids, the result of successive breeding and selection, provided the genetic base from which modern hybrids have been raised, and a few, despite changes in taste and modern advances, are still worthy of a place in any good garden, after more than half a century. In this respect 'August Orange' and 'Dauntless' come to mind, both having numerous long-lasting flowers.

In 1941 Stout published an article in *Herbertia* entitled 'Memorandum On A Monograph Of the Genus *Hemerocallis*'. Sadly, due to his sudden death, it was his last article and it was not until 1968 that a monograph on day lilies appeared. It was published by the American Horticultural Society as the *Day Lily Handbook*. In it Dr Hu Stated: 'This is not the time for making radical changes in the nomenclature and classification of *Hemerocallis*.' Now, two decades later, the time has come for a revision of the classification, since the Species Working Party of the AHS (American Hemerocallis Society) has decided which of the various species should be grouped together, or are in fact conspecific. Another reason is that it would be in line with the general reclassification of lily-like plants proposed by Dahlgren and Yeo. In their revision *Hemerocallis* is placed in a family of its own.

But let us return to the 1940s. Even before World War II the Henry Field Seed Company had sponsored flower shows. Once the war was over Mary Anderson, who had organised the *Hemerocallis* round robins, planned to hold a 'Hem Show'. In this she was supported by Helen Field Fisher, the 'Flower Lady', who had had 27 years' experience with her own radio programme for gardeners. She was also a day lily enthusiast. They decided to organise a *Hemerocallis* Show in Shenandoah, Iowa, to be held on 13th July 1946. Invitations were both posted and broadcast. Potential visitors were asked to bring picnic hampers and sleeping bags as well as their flowers.

The response was quite overwhelming. Visitors came not just from the surrounding states, but from all over the USA. Some VIPs attended and the following day, on 14th July, a society for *Hemerocallis* enthusiasts was founded. It was called the 'Midwest Hemerocallis Society', membership fee three US dollars. Even in the year of its foundation the society had 757 members. The first yearbook, intended for an estimated membership of only 600, was immediately oversubscribed. The membership potential was not confined solely to the Midwest; there were enquiries from states and countries further afield. Therefore, at a meeting in Bartlesville, Oklahoma in 1949, where 300 exhibits were shown, participants agreed to change the name to the 'Hemerocallis Society'. They also agreed to award an annual prize for the best variety; in the following year the first prizewinner of what became known as the 'Stout Medal' was the hybrid *Hesperus*.

A trials garden was created in 1950 and maintained by the Henry Field Seed Company; a register was issued in which 2,695 types from 17 growers were listed. In addition to the Stout Medal a popularity poll was also instituted for the most popular variety of the year. The first winner of this was 'Painted Lady', which went on to win the Stout Medal in 1951. More about this will be found in the chapter entitled 'Propagation and Selection of Hybrids', where more details are given about the awards of the AHS. In 1955 a resolution was passed adding the word 'American' to the title of the society. Today membership stands at well over 3,000. Apart from its role in displaying, adjudicating and awarding prizes to outstanding varieties, the Society is also the international registration authority for day lilies, registering new types. Even beginners are encouraged to register their hybrids (see pages 107–9). Registration in effect copyrights the names of the hybrids.

Europe in the Twentieth Century

When one recalls that Europe was the first destination of day lilies from China and Japan, it is surprising that the plant is not better known in Europe. And indeed, most of the plants that are grown in European gardens are American hybrids; very few are European hybrids. Day lilies in Europe developed along quite different lines from those in America.

Charles (Karl Ludwig) Sprenger and Willy Müller have already been mentioned and there will be further references to them. In an article for the German Iris and Lily Society in 1967 the latter recalled his years in Naples from 1900 to 1907. His uncle, Charles Sprenger, had rented the Villa Lamantina on Vomero, the highest mountain in the area; the grounds included an old quarry. Here Sprenger and Müller created a private botanic garden, 'Hortus Vomerensis', where they grew many day lilies, including some that were at that time not very common:

H. minor, *H. graminea*, *H. thunbergii*, *H. lilioasphodelus* and *H. middendorffii*. They omitted *H. fulva* and the variety *disticha* since these are sterile and of little use for breeding.

They raised and introduced several varieties, but unfortunately, as record-keeping was not considered important in those days, the parentage of most of them is not known. Most have been superseded. Stout mentions *H.* × *elmensis*, *H.* × *hippeastroides* and *H. vomerensis*, for example, though these have long since disappeared. Later hybrids were more successful following the further introductions of Father Giraldi from the province of Shen-shi in China in 1904.

Among the new plants were *H. citrina* and *H. maculata*, which was soon recognised as a variety of *H. fulva*. These plants turned out to be wonderful parents, regularly producing abundant seeds. Thus *H. thunbergii* × *H. citrina* produced, among others, *H. ochroleuca*, an enlarged *H. thunbergii*, *H.* × *baroni*, which looked more like *H. citrina*, and *H.* × *mülleri*, which takes after both parents equally. *H. aurantiaca* 'Major' × *H. citrina* produced 'Ajax'; 'Ajax' × *H. citrina* produced 'Sir Michael Forster'; and from *H. fulva* var. *maculata* × *H. citrina* came the hybrid *H.* × *fulcitrina*.

In another shipment of plants, this time from Father Cypriani, there was a fulva clone that was smaller than previously known fulva forms. This received the name *H. fulva* 'Cypriani'. However, the eruption of Mount Vesuvius during the night of Palm Sunday in 1906 caused much destruction to the Vomero collection, and since the paths of uncle and nephew had also diverged by this time (Sprenger had become director of the Achilleion Garden in Corfu) Müller decided to move to Nocera Inferiore. If further hybrids were produced, there is no record of them, though we do know that Müller exchanged plants with someone of the same name as himself, who was the director of the Botanical Gardens in Strasbourg and was studying the problem of sterility in *H. fulva*.

During the two World Wars in Europe there was understandably little interest in day lilies, and it was not until 1945 that work recommenced. Max Steiger, a German dentist, found the propagation of irises and day lilies so fascinating that he eventually gave up his practice and moved to Tenerife, where climatic conditions were particularly suitable. Here it was possible to raise flourishing plants within nine to 14 months of sowing the seeds. Unfortunately Steiger died not long after emigrating. Many of the hybrids he raised are known to us only by name, 'Lagerfeuer' and 'Zitrone' for instance, but they were not really up to today's standards.

Apart from the German breeders there were also some outstanding British breeders. The first of these and, indeed, the pioneer of day lily breeding, was schoolmaster George Yeld (1845–1953), who eventually retired to Gerrard's Cross in Buckinghamshire. Whilst teaching in York, he raised day lilies and irises as a hobby. He began breeding day lilies in 1877 using several varieties of *H. fulva* and *H. lilioasphodelus* that were already in the garden; he obtained *H. dumortieri* and *H. middendorffii* from York Nurseries and *H.*

graminea and *H. minor* from Messrs. Fisher, Son and Sibray of Sheffield. His first hybrid to be registered, in fact the first day lily hybrid ever registered, was 'Apricot' (*H. lilioasphodelus* × *middendorffii*), which received an Award of Merit from the Royal Horticultural Society in 1893. 'Apricot' was introduced by Pritchards of Riverslea Nurseries, Christchurch, Dorset in 1913 in their autumn catalogue No. 23. Yeld's hybrid 'Sovereign' was also introduced by Pritchards in the same year, under the synonym 'Beauty' (it has no connection with a cultivar called 'Sovereign', which is distributed in Europe). His 'J.S. Gaynor', a fine orange-yellow, was introduced by Pritchards in 1928 and was much used by breeders in the United States in the late 1940s and 1950s. Other hybrids of Yeld's that are still grown today include 'Pioneer', 'Gold Dust' and 'Estmere'. Also important were his hybrids 'Miniken', a small yellow (*lilioasphodelus* crossed with *nana*) and 'Moidore'. He also used *H. aurantiaca* as the pollen parent crossing into *H. thunbergii* to create 'Chrysolite', 'Halo' and 'Golden Bell'.

A friend and colleague of George Yeld, Amos Perry, began hybridising day lilies in 1885. He lived from 1871 to 1953 and the whole of his working life was spent in horticulture and the nursery that he founded, Perry's Hardy Plant Farm at Enfield, Middlesex, became famous throughout the world. It survived two World Wars, periods when ornamental plants were ruthlessly sacrificed to provide ground for food crops. When nearing his retirement, he compiled a plant diary known as *Perry's Diary*, which is essentially a record of the plants he raised between 1894 and 1945. There is a comprehensive section on his *Hemerocallis* hybrids. The diary was printed privately and only a few copies are still in existence, but at a time when few growers kept proper records it was an act of great foresight and provides invaluable material for students of the genus.

Amos Perry began his hybridising work on day lilies early in his career, at about the same time as George Yeld, using the species *H. fulva*, *lilioasphodelus*, *thunbergii* and, later, *H. citrina*. His first recorded cross was 'Amos Perry' (*citrina* × *lilioasphodelus*), which was introduced in 1902. He later concentrated on trying to create red day lilies from *H. fulva* and *multiflora* and did much to produce day lilies for the smaller garden. He was inspired by a splendid example of *H. fulva* 'Kwanso', but did not have much success with *H. fulva* until eventually he came across *H. fulva* 'Cypriani', which was fertile. From this he raised his well-known 'Margaret Perry' in 1920, one of which he was most proud, and, five years later, 'Yellow Hammer'. 'E.A. Bowles' also pleased him, as did 'George Yeld' (*thunbergii* × *H. fulva* 'Cypriani'), which was selected from many thousands of seedlings by George Yeld himself during a visit in 1922, and named to perpetuate his memory. Amos Perry named many day lilies after members of his family (*H*. 'Thelma Perry') as well as after famous people ('Byng of Vimy'); a large number also bore place names ('Chingford', 'Totnes').

His exhibit of day lilies at the Royal Horticultural Society's Flower Show in July 1941 caused much interest and earned him a Silver Gilt Lindley

Medal. It is said that Perry raised a white-flowered day lily, but, if so, it has been lost to cultivation. When Perry retired, half his stock was taken over by Dandy Easton of Meare Close Nurseries, Tadworth, Surrey.

Among the post-war British day lily breeders mention must be made of Leonard Brummitt, who died in April 1981. Although irises and orchids were his main interest, in the 1950s and mid-1960s he introduced a wide selection of day lilies. He strove particularly to produce hardy red hybrids (*H.* 'Cherry Ripe'), but his strains can generally be recognised by the prefix 'Banbury', a small town in Oxfordshire where he lived. He produced, among others, 'Banbury Canary', which was awarded an FCC,* and 'Banbury Cinnamon', which gained an AM† in the early 1980s after trial at Wisley.

Harry Randall was another iris breeder who, through his American connections, became interested in day lilies and began hybridising them from plants he had received from well-known American breeders Hubert Fischer and Orville Fay. His best-known day lilies were again named after places near where he lived at Beaconsfield, Buckinghamshire: 'Amersham' FCC, a rich velvety-orange tetraploid flushed deep red, tinged green at the base, and 'Missenden' FCC, a large funnel-shaped tetraploid with deep, rich, velvety, red flowers flushed black, yellowish-orange at the base, which was most effective close to. Although both 'Amersham' and 'Missenden' are considered superior to the popular 'Stafford', they are surprisingly little known as garden plants.

Just as Brummitt and Randall were retiring from the scene, Robert Coe, formerly a farmer and later professional nurseryman of Norton Hall, Cold Norton, Essex, began to register his first hybrids. Again much of his original stock came from American sources. He was a specialist grower of irises, kniphofia and, to a lesser extent, eremurus. In 1970 Norton Hall Nurseries was awarded the first Gold Medal for an exhibition of day lilies at the Royal Horticultural Society's Show at Westminster.

Coe selected his day lilies primarily for hardiness and several, such as 'Norton Hall', 'Norton Orange' and 'Norton Tallboy', are still to be found in collections and nurseries, more frequently in Europe than in his native Britain, although there are remnants of his collection in several gardens in the Essex area. Much of his stock was later taken over by the nurseryman Lissaman, but it has now been dispersed to various collectors. The day lilies with the Norton prefix were mainly, though not entirely, tetraploids. Generally speaking they were not too satisfactory, because the flowers frequently did not open properly – the tepals were very thick. Certainly growth was vigorous and the foliage larger and broader. Many of his diploids have stood the test of time, in particular *H.* 'Lemon Bells' FCC, a very floriferous light lemon-yellow, but one of his best tetraploids is the clear pink 'Elaine Strutt', which is enjoying a resurgence of popularity and has none of the tetraploid faults. It may soon become more freely available as it is undergoing trials for

---

*FCC = First Class Certificate
†AM = Award of Merit

micropropagation. Coe used 'Buzz Bomb' crossed with another red, 'Bess Ross', to produce 'Jet Scarlet' and 'Red Precious' AM, two very good bright reds suitable for smaller gardens. He also attempted to raise a white-flowered variety, but the nearest he got was 'Snow Fairy', a small-flowered white with an intense orange throat, and 'White Emeralds', which had a greenish tinge. A collection of Coe hybrids is being amassed as part of one of the National Hemerocallis Reference Collections by the Leeds Parks Department in Yorkshire under the curatorship of Gordon Cooper.

When Coe had to relinquish the nursery at Norton Hall, he began a new programme of hybridising at his small property at nearby Panfield, prefixing some of these day lilies with 'Panfield', e.g. 'Panfield Charm', 'Panfield Dazzle' and 'Panfield Plum'. Others raised at about the same time included 'Gold Lace', 'Shot Silk' and 'Lavender Mink'. Some of these are growing in the Day Lily Display Garden at Apple Court in Hampshire, but the majority of these later hybrids are in the hands of his son, Philip Coe. In 1974 Coe registered the brilliant red 'Bruno Muller', one of his last and one of his best.

Other British day lily breeders of note were Leslie Cave of Thames Ditton, whose 'Jane Graham' was awarded an AM in 1980 after trial, Peter Barr of Taplow, Berks., Ernest Ladham of Elstead, Surrey and R. Wallace of Tunbridge Wells, Kent.

At the 1963 International Horticultural Show in Hamburg, day lilies, including 75 new varieties from America, were given their first real exposure to a wider general public. The gold medal was won by 'Finest Hour', which has since been more or less forgotten, whereas the silver medallists, 'Corky' and 'Golden Chimes', are still rated highly and grown in many gardens. Max Steiger, who was mentioned earlier, also received distinctions for 'Feuervogel', 'Margarite' and 'Stern von Rio'. The 1980s saw the formation of three more societies with considerable interest in day lilies: the 'Vlaamse Irisvereniging' in Belgium, the 'British Hosta and Hemerocallis Society' and the 'Australian Hemerocallis Society'.

Trends in Recent Years

Recent years have seen a considerable growth of interest in day lilies. This has in part been fostered by national and international horticultural shows, as well as garden festivals, and by the trials gardens of several nurseries. Interest is also stimulated by the plantings of day lilies in gardens open to the public, such as at Wisley; the National Hemerocallis Reference Collections at Leeds Parks Department; Epsom and Ewell Parks Department; and Little Hermitage, St Catherine's Down (Isle of Wight), all in the United Kingdom. Francois Verhaert has amassed a very large collection of modern American hybrids in his Display Garden at Zandhoven, Belgium. His observations will be invaluable. It is really only by seeing the plants displayed that their beauty can be appreciated.

Sadly most people still think of the day lily in terms of the common dull orange, *H. fulva*, which is scarcely likely to arouse much interest. However, once people become aware of the great variety of colours and shapes to be found in modern day lilies, their interest starts to increase. But trials gardens have another function. Day lilies are now being bred not only in Europe, but also in America, New Zealand and Australia, and inevitably some are more tender than others: some indeed are bred for near-tropical climates and will not flower in temperate zones. Trials gardens can tell you, where glossy catalogues often do not, which varieties will flourish in your particular part of the world.

THE SPECIES

Place in the Plant Kingdom

People often think that lilies and day lilies are very closely related and that therefore day lilies, like lilies, grow from bulbs. This is not the case. Nor are the roots strictly tubers or rhizomes. Rather, some of the roots are swollen and may act as storage organs. Nor are lilies and day lilies particularly closely related, though, if you look them up in a plant dictionary, you will probably find them both together under the Liliaceae family.

Recent investigations have led to the complete reorganisation of the Liliaceae order. Most of the botanists who support this reorganisation feel that *Hemerocallis* should be given the status of Family, and this is how it was dealt with by Dahlgren and Yeo, whose reorganisation is now generally accepted. They place the day lilies, *Hemerocallis*, in the family Hemerocallidaceae.

The following are the main differences between lilies and day lilies. First of all there is the shape of the seed: black and round (or ovoid) in *Hemerocallis*, flat and brown with only a thin skin in lilies. In day lilies the nectaries are situated in the walls of the ovary (septal nectaries), whereas in lilies they are at the base of the perigonial leaves. Lastly the day lily has roots, some of which are storage organs, whereas the lily has a scaly bulb.

The name of the genus, *Hemerocallis*, was given them by Linnaeus and is made up from the Greek words for 'beauty' and 'day' and so expresses the idea of 'beauty for a day'. Linnaeus knew of two types of day lily, the yellow and the tawny or fulvous day lily. In 1753 he gave the yellow day lily the name *H. lilioasphodelus* fonna *lutea* and regarded the tawny day lily simply as a variant, calling it fonna *fulva*. In the second edition of his *Species Plantarum* he corrected himself and so in 1762 the plant received its own name, *H. fulva*.

The name *H. fulva* is still valid, but that of *H. flava* has been changed to *H. lilioasphodelus* in line with the rule of priority. As Hylander was able to show, the species had already been described by Pena and Lobel in 1570 under the name *Asphodelus luteus liliflorus*. Linnaeus had unwittingly allowed an error to creep in when he changed the name and this had repercussions later (see p. 51). As the change of name was carried out by Hylander, the plant is now called '*H. lilioasphodelus* L. emend. Hylander' (emend. = altered by). However, this revamped old name has not yet been generally adopted, even though Dress confirmed it in 1955.

Apart from this there are few synonyms among *Hemerocallis*, something that should make life easier for botanists. Unfortunately, the plant that one actually sees in the botanical gardens of Europe or America does not always correspond with the original species. Therefore it is necessary to compare and to establish which plants in fact represent the original descriptions.

Physical Characteristics

Roots
As a rule the roots of day lilies are tapering, spindle-shaped swellings that may not penetrate too deeply. The appearance of the roots is diagnostic for the different species. The roots may form pseudobulbs, as in *H. citrina*, which sometimes even stand vertically, as in *H. altissima*. Sometimes the roots thicken only near their ends, as in *H. minor* and *H. nana* (which indicates that they are related), or else these fleshy swellings are more compact and the edible root nodules can be harvested. Often the roots are cylindrical, as in *H. dumortieri*, or occasionally spindle-shaped, as in the ubiquitous *H. fulva*. On the other hand *H. lilioasphodelus*, *H. fulva* var. *littorea* and *H. middendorffii* have fibrous root systems. The colour of the roots varies from white through a yellowish colour to a reddish-brown.

Crown
By crown we mean that part of the plant that forms the transition between the roots and the leaves. The crown forms the 'heart' of the plant. Here the scapes and buds begin to form at the end of the growing period of one year, ready for the next. This is also the vulnerable part where damage can cause the death of the plant (see crown rot, p. 126). As the point of intitiation of the plant's growth it is of great interest to propagators (see Lanoline-BAP-IAA-method p. 116).

Foliage
The 'fan' of leaves gets its name, naturally enough, from the way the leaves are arranged above the crown, rising in two compact ranks. The leaves are grass-like and can vary from very narrow to as much as 4cm wide, but generally they are about half that width. They tend to be folded along the midrib. The foliage may stand erect, arch outwards, or be bent over near the tips of the leaves (reflexed or recurved). Many species lie dormant in the winter when the leaves die back, but there are also evergreen types. By crossing plants of the latter sort with winter-hardy ones, semi-evergreen hybrids can be obtained, whose behaviour will depend on prevailing conditions.

Scapes
The round scapes or flower stalks vary in length from 4cm (*H. darrowiana*) to

THE SPECIES

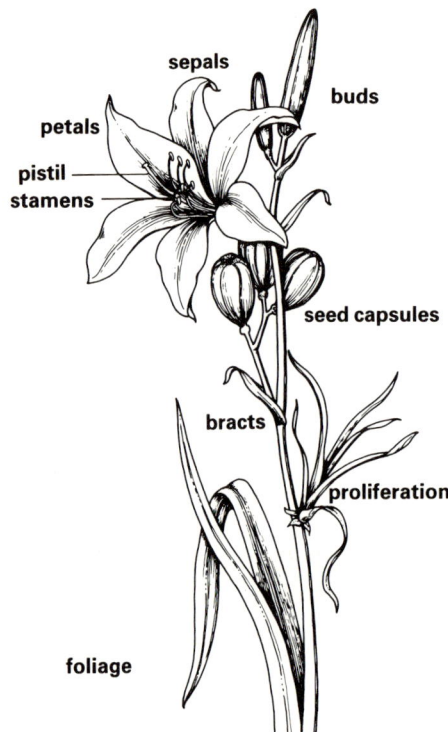

Figure 4 Morphology of *Hemerocallis*. It is usual, but not strictly correct, to make a distinction between sepals and petals.

200cm (*H. altissima*). They may grow erect, or be arched or bowed down towards the ground under the weight of their blooms, as with *H. multiflora*. As a rule the scapes branch several times within the top third of their length. Sometimes, as in *H. dumortieri* and *H. middendorffii*, this branching occurs only at the very tip of the stem. One species does not branch at all and carries a solitary bloom per scape; this is *H. nana*.

Proliferations

Occasionally one may notice a small leaf fan forming on the flower scape. This is known as a proliferation (an axillary or side shoot). It can be removed from the parent plant and used for propagation.

Bracts

These are like small leaves subtending the branches of the flower scapes. There is just one bract at the base of each branch. As a rule the bract is longish, lanceolate or an elongated oval running to an extended point. With *H. middendorffii* this point tends to be shortish and the bract generally has a broader, oval shape. In this case, because they are situated at the tip of the scape, they also overlap one another. The shapes of the bracts and the way they are arranged can be used to show how the individual species are related.

Flowers

The perianth, the showy, colourful part of the flower, consists of six segments. These are arranged in threes, one set above the other. The three outer segments are usually narrower and more pointed at the tip than the inner ones and are called sepals; above these lie the three petals. From the botanical point of view, this description is actually not quite correct: one should really talk in terms of inner and outer 'tepals'. However, even among botanists, it is now common usage to differentiate as between sepals and petals where these can be clearly distinguished as separate whorls. In *Hemerocallis* the sepals/petals are, to a greater or lesser degree, united at the base so as to form a tube. The segments may be strongly bent back at their tips (reflexed or recurved), or they may be straight, and if they are straight they will form funnel-shaped or trumpet-shaped flowers. The natural colours of the blooms range from yellow through orange and reddish-brown to near-red. There are also doubles, as for instance *H. fulva* 'Kwanso'.

Duration

Each flower of a day lily normally blooms for just one day and there is a succession of flowers throughout the flowering season. The opening and closing of the individual flowers may occur at different times according to type. Some open in the evening and close the following night (long or extended blooming). Others, having bloomed overnight, will close as early as the next morning (nocturnal). Sometimes the species blooms from morning to evening, as is generally the case with hybrids (diurnal).

Reproductive Organs

Day lilies are monoclinous, that is to say both sexes occur within the same flower. The male sex organ, the stamen, consists of six long filaments, mainly of a yellow colour, each terminating in an anther, which contains the pollen. When they are closed, the anthers are yellow or sometimes greyish in colour. They burst a few hours after the flower has opened and expose the pollen. The pistil forming the female organ is noticeably longer than the filaments and consists of a stigma, which is connected through the style to the ovary within the perianth tube. The stigma itself consists of three small bulbous thickenings that exude a sticky substance during the optimum period of pollination. Occasionally the stigma has three slits, but this feature is not typical. In the ovary there can be as many as 42 ovules, but not all of these develop; consequently the actual number of possible seeds is considerably fewer. With tetraploid types there may be only eight to eleven seeds that eventually ripen.

Seed Capsules

When the seeds are ripe, the seed capsules are either roundish or an elongated elliptical shape. They have six ribs and these snap open in pairs when the capsules are ripe. Inside the capsule are three rows of black seeds that are either round or elliptical, with a small raised point. The number of seeds depends on whether the species is diploid or tetraploid. It takes 60–80 days from fertilisation of the ovules to full ripeness of the seeds.

Classification

To date the only classification of *Hemerocallis* is that proposed by Stout in his *Day Lilies*, published in 1934. He separated those with branched scapes from those without branches. The first group he called Euhemera and the second Dihemera. He considered that only *H. dumortieri* and *H. middendorffii* belong to this latter group, and excluded *H. nana* which, as is well known, also has scapes that do not branch. Stout's proposed division was not accepted and no-one now supports it.

THE SPECIES

In my view there are five main groups of day lily and the members within each group are either related or are perhaps varieties of one another.

1 Fulva Group
The roots of these plants have spindle-shaped swellings. The blooms contain a brownish-red (fulvous) dye. (*H. aurantiaca* 'Major' does not contain this dye, which suggests that it is unlikely to be a variety of this species.)

> H. aurantiaca
> H. fulva

2 Citrina Group
The scapes are branched. The blooms open in the evening or at night and are fragrant. They are mostly yellow and have long perianth tubes.

> H. altissima
> H. citrina
> H. coreana
> H. lilioasphodelus
> H. minor
> H. pedicellata
> H. thunbergii
> H. yezoensis

3 Middendorffii Group
The scapes are not branched. The bracts are mainly short and broad, but in any case they overlap. The blooms are orange.

> H. dumortieri
> H. esculenta
> H. exaltata
> H. hakunensis
> H. middendorffii

4 Nana Group
The scapes do not exceed 50cm in height. The perianth tube is shorter than 1cm. The veins in the perianth segments are not branched. The plant is not winter-hardy.

> H. forrestii
> H. nana

5 Multiflora Group
The scapes have many branches. The flowers are borne on short stalks and are smaller than 7cm, with tubes less than 2cm long.

> H. micrantha
> H. multiflora
> H. plicata

H. graminea is not quite so easy to place. According to the description it should belong to group 2. However, Stout knew of plants of this kind that bore a greater resemblance to those of group 3. It is therefore quite possible that two different species (or varieties) could have been given the same name. We do not yet possess any samples of *H. darrowiana*.

Identification Key to the Species

It is possible that some Korean and Japanese species may simply be varieties of *Hemerocallis* that are normally natives of China. An international working party of which the author is a member is at present wrestling with the problem of determining the status of the individual species.

THE SPECIES

Identification Key for Hemerocallis Species

1. Over-wintering habits:
1.1 Plants not winter-hardy, evergreen foliage. → 2
1.2 Plants winter-hardy, evergreen or dormant. → 3

2. Nana Group: scapes less than 50cm long, perianth tubes less than 1cm. Veins on flower segments non-branching. Orange-red flowers.
2.1 Scapes multiple branched with four to eight blooms.
 = *H. forrestii*
2.2 Scape unbranched with solitary flower. = *H. nana*

3. Colour of flower:
3.1 Brownish-red, diurnal → 4
3.2 Yellow or yellowish-orange, nocturnal or extended blooming, fragrant. → 5
3.3 Orange, diurnal. → 6

4. Fulva Group: the roots of the plants have spindle-shaped swellings. The flowers contain the fulvous dye typical of this group.
4.1 Winter-hardy with evergreen foliage. Blooms orange tinged with fulvous dye.
 = *H. aurantiaca*
4.2 Foliage dies back in winter. Flower colour varies considerably from orange to red, but always having a fulvous overcast. Numerous varieties and clones, including one with double flowers. = *H. fulva*

5. Citrina Group: the scapes are branched and the flowers open in the evening or during the night and are fragrant. As a rule the flowers are yellow and have noticeably long perianth tubes.
5.1 Trumpet-shaped yellow flowers on scapes 120–200cm tall. The plant overwinters as a conspicuous heap of foliage.
 = *H. altissima*
5.2 The broad widely-arching leaves are reddish at the base and the yellow flowers are set on scapes 90–110cm long. Perianth tubes one-third as long as the flowers. Self-sterile. = *H. citrina*
5.3 Flowers similar to above, but leaves narrow and upright and without red colouring at the base. Scapes 100–120cm tall. Very fertile. Obovate capsules.
 = *H. thunbergii*
5.4 Similar to above, but scapes shorter (80–90cm) and seed capsules ellipsoidal.
 = *H. yezoensis*
5.5 Yellow flowers conspicuously stalked and set on widely-branched scapes that overtop the 40cm high sweeping foliage by at least as much again.
 = *H. lilioasphodelus*
5.6 Branching occurs higher up the scape than with the previous type, but carries 50–80 yellow flowers with short pedicels.
 = *H. coreana*
5.7 The scape is bowed, not in excess of 60cm, has few branches and bears fewer than six yellow flowers. = *H. minor*
5.8 Similar to the previous one except that the flowers are orangey-yellow. = *H. pedicellata*

THE SPECIES

6. Branching Habits:
6.1 Entire or virtual absence of branching. → 7
6.2 Plant with simple or multiple branching. → 8

7. Middendorffii Group: the scapes are not branched. The bracts are mostly short, broad and overlapping each other.
7.1 The scape stands 90cm tall, is unbranched and extends well above the foliage. The flowers, which have tubes of only 12mm, are clustered. Reblooming. Seed capsules ellipsoidal.
= *H. middendorffii*

7.2 Resembles the previous type, but has perianth tubes of 2–3cm.
= *H. esculenta*

7.3 Again similar to the above, except that the tepals of the cup-shaped flowers are not curved back to the same extent as in the previous species. With its scape of 90–120cm, this is the tallest species of the group.
= *H. exaltata*

7.4 Scape with little or no branching, does not overtop foliage. Brownish flower buds, globose seed capsules. Early blooming, non reblooming. = *H. dumortieri*

7.5 Resembles previous species,

Figure 5 Growth habits and comparative sizes of *Hemerocallis* species (1).

THE SPECIES

except that the scape noticeably overtops the foliage. Seed capsules broadly elliptical with erect lobes.   = *H. hakunensis*

7.6 Also similar to *H. dumortieri*. The bracts, which are lanceolate and 5cm in length, turn brown soon after florescence.
= *H. graminea*

8. Multiflora Group: branched scapes. Flowers have stalks and are not in excess of 7cm, with tubes of no more than 2cm length.

8.1 Scape scantily branched with up to four blooms. Flower segments narrow.   = *H. micrantha*

8.2 Scape irregularly branched bearing from five to eleven trumpet-shaped flowers.
= *H. plicata*

8.3 Scape with multiple branching bearing up to 100 flowers with opened out tepals.
= *H. multiflora*

Description of the Species

H. altissima (Stout 1943)

This plant has numerous coarse-fibred roots with spindle-shaped swellings. They are swollen at their ends with erect pseudobulbs. The

35

Figure 6 *Hemerocallis altissima.*

medium-coarse foliage grows fanned out and erect. The individual leaves can be from 60 to 120cm in length and 20–25mm across. When they turn yellow in the autumn, they become tough and the plant over-winters as a mere heap of foliage. The scapes are erect and can attain a height of about 2m; they are branched in the upper quarter of their length. The leaf-like bracts are from 7 to 10cm long and begin to turn brown almost as soon as the first flower buds open.

The trumpet-shaped flowers have a diameter of about 7.5cm. The perianth tube is noticeably long at 5cm. The bright yellow flowers are fragrant and the species is nocturnal, the flowers opening in the late afternoon and fading the following morning. The seed capsules are egg-shaped and attached by the more pointed end. When these are fully ripe they are about 2cm long and about the same width.

Robert Coe, the British day lily breeder, stated in 1958 that *H. altissima* flourished along the lower course of the River Yangtse. But this is strange since no wild day lilies grow in this area. It is possible, however, that the species might have been cultivated there and/or have escaped from cultivation. The seeds that Dr A.N. Steward sent to America probably came from peasants of this area. The original plants come from the Purple Mountains near Nanking. The species flowers from mid-July until September and sometimes even later.

H. aurantiaca (Baker 1890)

The dark green leaves are about 75cm long. They are robust and stand six to eight in each rank. They rise up straight at first and then arch right over. The leaves are between 12 and 20mm wide. The scape carrying the blooms grows to about 90cm long and is slightly arched; it is very thick and branches only near the tip. The plant has leaf-like bracts at nodes in the upper third of the scape as well as subtending the branches; they are lanceolate in shape with a long point that lies closely along the scape. The six to eight blooms that the species produces have either short stalks (pedicels) or none at all. It is diurnal, the flowers opening during the day. They are orange with a reddish tinge on the outside, and they glisten noticeably in sunlight. The diameter of the flower is 13cm; sepals and petals are more or less the same size, 7.5cm long and 2.5cm about the plant in 1958, claimed that it grew wild in the area around Mt Ibuki in Japan. However, a number of Japanese botanists dispute this, and in 1965, Ohwi, writing in *Japanese Flora* stated that *H. aurantiaca* was a species from China seldom cultivated in Japan.

It is a rarity in gardens and is seldom offered commercially. Nevertheless it has much to commend it, for, as Sprenger discovered in 1903, it bloomed in Naples from April until November, making it the longest-blooming of species.

Synonyms: *H. aurantiaca* var. *littorea* (Nakai 1932) = synonym for *H. fulva* var. *littorea*.

Figure 7 *Hemerocallis aurantiaca.*

broad, with the latter having a slightly wavy edge. The cylindrical perianth tube is about 3cm in length. The stamens are approximately half the length of the petals and the anthers are dark grey. The seed capsules are longish, 4.5cm long and 2.5cm in cross-section, blunt at the end.

H. aurantiaca is the only semi-evergreen species. When used for hybridising, its offspring are invariably fully evergreen. Baker, who named it from plants growing at Kew, thought that it came originally from Japan, though others say that it arose as a chance seedling at Kew. Coe, who made some enquiries

H. aurantiaca 'Major' (Baker 1895)

The title 'Major' does not refer to the height to which this plant grows, since at only 60cm it is distinctly smaller than the foregoing, but rather to the size of its blooms. These resemble those of *H. aurantiaca*, but are bigger, and of a fuller and more even orange colour without the reddish tinge. The flowers do not open all that wide, so that the perianth is only 12cm across. The sepals are 8.5cm long by 2.5cm wide, while the measurements of the petals are 10cm and 3.5cm respectively.

Baker himself suspected that this clone was really no more than an accidental mutant seedling and not a true variant. In 1930 Bayley expressed some doubt as to whether it was even related to *H. aurantiaca*. Stout was similarly minded and suggested in 1941 that it should be separated from the main species. Earlier, in 1903, Mallet considered this 'the most beautiful plant of the entire genus'. He reported that the British flower-bulb merchant, R. Wallace, while travelling around Japan, had blooms from such a plant set before him as a salad. Thereupon he apparently reached an agreement with his host to sell him all his plants, which were growing among *Iris kaempferi*. This type blooms in July and occasionally still has a few flowers in September, but it does not set any seeds.

Synonyms: *H.* × *baroni* (Sprenger 1903) = hybrid from *H. thunbergii* × *H. citrina*, very similar to the latter.

H. citrina (Baroni 1897)

H. citrina is a plant of compact growth whose roots have many stubby, club-shaped swellings, which in turn develop lateral branches. The dark green leaves are coarse-fibred, semi-erect and die back in the autumn. The length of the leaves varies from about 75cm to 110cm and they are 3.5cm wide. In sunlight they have a blue-green sheen. The stiff, erect scapes can reach a height of about 1m; they are brittle and branch in the upper quarter. The number of flowers varies from seven to 65!

The species has pale lemon-yellow flowers and blooms at night. The slender trumpets vary from 12 to 17cm in length, of which 3–5cm make up the tube. The sepals are greenish on the outside, purple at their tips and indented. They are 2cm wide, whereas the petals are 2.5cm wide and have wavy edges. Moreover, both display a network of veins. The seed capsules, which are up to 3cm long, are more triangular than round in section, and blunt and indented at the end. The black seeds are hemispherical and irregularly ribbed.

Figure 8 *Hemerocallis citrina.*

According to Baroni this species grows wild in China in the province of Shen-shi. An Italian missionary who had settled there sent him a specimen in 1895. A wider distribution for the species was later claimed by Charles Sprenger and his nephew Willy Müller, who carried on the work begun by his uncle. Most of the plants of *H. citrina* in gardens came originally from Müller and are unfortunately not the right plant. Usually they turn out to be *H. thunbergii*. The species is worth growing for its lemony scent, and it is in the hope of passing on this scent that it is often used for hybridising, though the flowers of its hybrids often have the disadvantage of fading and wilting on hot, dry days. Stout found *H. citrina* to be self-sterile. Although the pollen tube grows through the style following self-pollination, it fails to initiate fertilisation.

H. citrina var. vespertina [(Hara) Erhardt 1988]

This plant was originally described in 1941 by Hara, a Japanese botanist, under the title *H. vespertina*. Subsequent authorities, Dr Hu among them, consider it *nomen illegitimum*, since they say it does not differ materially from *H. thunbergii*. The American Hemerocallis Society's Species Working Party now believes that it can put forward proof that this is in fact a distinct species, or at least a variety.

Plants of this species that grow in my garden have been raised from seed and have not so far flowered, though they are growing strongly. J. Schabell, who received his seeds directly from Japan, described the plants in a letter: 'The scapes are very strong and tall, reaching 180cm. Some of them branch up to seven times, as well as having terminal branches, so that one finds mature plants with as many as 75 buds per scape. The clear light yellow blooms have a diameter of about 7.5cm and a faint fragrance.'

This very large number of buds ensures a very long flowering period, beginning in July and lasting, in suitable weather, until October. It seems to form the link between *H. citrina* and *H. altissima*.

H. coreana (Nakai 1932)

The roots of this plant spread horizontally. The leaves are 12–45cm long and up to 45mm wide. The scape, which is between 50 and 80cm tall, has numerous branches at the apex. In contrast to the more lanceolate lower bracts the upper ones are ovoid. The short-stemmed flowers appear wax-like and are greenish-yellow. The perianth tube can be up to 5cm long and the segments extend another 7cm, the sepals being 13mm and the petals 25mm wide. The seed capsules are 2.5cm long and 1cm wide, looking distinctly long.

Nakai states that he found plants of this species in Korea as well as Japan and China. There is, however, still some doubt as to whether all the

Figure 9 *Hemerocallis coreana*.

plants in these different locations are the same. Dr Hu has identified plant material from the Korean strain partly as *H. lilioasphodelus* and partly as *H. minor*, while Ohwi sees similarities between the Japanese samples and *H. yezoensis*. Genuine plant material has reached America, but regrettably the species is not yet grown in Europe. This is a pity, for the scapes carry between 50 and 80 flowers each. It is on account of the number of flowers that R.H. Kitchingman proposed its inclusion in the *multiflora* group; on the other hand, I feel that the long perianth tubes argue against this. For a definitive resolution of this problem we must wait until it has been established whether *H. coreana* is nocturnal or not.

Figure 10 *Hemerocallis darrowiana*.

Synonyms: *H. crocea* (Lamarck 1799) = synonym for *H. fulva* Linnaeus 1762.

H. darrowiana (Hu 1969)

This is a miniature species growing to no more than 10 or 14cm high. The outer foliage curls, whereas the inner leaves are more erect and sword-like. They are 5–8cm long and 2–8mm wide. A single scape between 1 and 4cm in length rises from the short rank of leaves and bears two flowers, each of which has a diameter of about 6cm. The yellow flower segments are 4cm long and the tube 2cm. The flowers resemble those of the genus *Zephyranthes*.

On 21st June 1969, during her Asian expedition, Dr Hu found this plant in the park of the National Science Museum in Tokyo, where various day lilies are grown. Her enquiries revealed that this day lily had been found by H. Sase on Sakhalin Island and that at that time it was still unnamed. The name eventually chosen for it was that of Dr Darrow, a former chairman of the Scientific Committee of the American Hemerocallis Society. Because Sakhalin has belonged to the Soviet Union since World War II, it has been and still is extraordinarily difficult to obtain further plant material, but efforts continue.

Synonyms: *H. disticha* (Donahue et David 1825) = synonym for *H. fulva* var. *disticha* Baker 1874.

H. dumortieri (Morren 1834)

This is also a very compact and low-growing plant, reaching 15–60cm in height. The leaves grow stiffly erect, six to eight in a rank. They are about 45cm long and generally 15–25mm wide, tapering a little towards the

Figure 11   *Hemerocallis dumortieri*.

gardens in Belgium, where they were described and drawn by Morren, who taught botany at the University of Ghent. The drawing shows the same narrow, grass-like foliage as that described by Mallet in 1903; in actual fact the leaves are somewhat wider.

The wide distribution of seeds has led to the development of several clones. There are, for instance, Perry's var. *rutilans* (1929) and Pearce's var. *altaica* (1952). These are, however, not genuine varieties but rather garden varieties. Also incorrect is the name *H. dumortierii* with two 'i's, which Bailey used.

Synonyms: *H. × elmensis* (Sprenger 1903) = hybrid from *H. minor × H. thunbergii*, according to Willy Müller; described by his uncle, Charles Sprenger, as a cross between *H. minor × H. citrina*.

H. esculenta (Koidzumi 1925)

The roots spread out widely, but do not manifest any obvious swellings. The foliage is in ranks of eight to 13 leaves, each 50–80cm long and 2–3cm wide. They arch and have papillae along their edges. The membranous bracts often do not occur until after the first branching of the scape and are 2.5cm in length. The scape is 60–90cm long and branches only near the tip.

The five or six trumpet-shaped flowers are borne on decidedly short pedicels, each sheathed in a short, oval bract. The flower segments are 7–8cm long and 3–4cm wide and, together with its tube of 2–3cm, the overall length can be as much as 11cm. The elongated seed capsules have flattened and indented ends.

end. The slender scape rises at a slight angle from the centre of the fan. From two to four flowers are arranged in pairs at its apex, their short pedicels covered by two overlapping basal bracts.

The flower buds show brownish-red on the outside, but the open flowers are orange. The blooms are bell-shaped with elongated oval segments and a short tube. The sepals are 45–55mm long and 6–12mm wide; the petals are 12–18mm wide and slightly reflexed. The seed capsule is obovate, 25mm long and 18mm in diameter.

The plant is widespread in Japan, Korea, Manchuria and eastern Siberia. The Japanese name for it is 'Hime-Kanzo' and it was from Japan that Siebold brought the first specimens to Holland in 1830. From Holland they found their way into

Figure 12 *Hemerocallis esculenta*.

When ripe they have a length of 2.5cm. The egg-shaped seeds have a diameter of 6mm.

The species is a native of the moutain meadows of the temperate regions of Japan from Hokkaido to Kyoto, as well as of Sakhalin Island. Japanese botanists have doubts as to whether this is really a true species, although their opinions as to its real identity vary. Koidzumi regards the plant as a form of *H. thunbergii*, while Ohwi, according to a statement in 1965, considers it to be a variety of *H. middendorffii*. In my garden I have the latter and also *H. exaltata* and *H. esculenta*, and I have formed the opinion that these three should at least belong in the same group; in connection with this, I should say that *H. exaltata* is closer to *H. middendorffii* than the species under discussion here, which has longer bracts and a noticeable branching of the scape.

H. exaltata (Stout 1934)

This species has robust folded foliage and a compact crown. Some of the roots are short and enlarged; others long, with spindle-shaped tuberous ends. It also has rhizomes that tend to spread. The sturdy leaves grow to 90cm in length, but the strong, thick scape rising to 120cm far overtops them, branching only at its apex. The bracts are a broad oval shape and 3cm long.

The bright orange blooms open during the day in June and July and are 12cm in diameter. The petals (i.e. the inner whorl of segments) are spatulate. The elliptical seed capsules are 3.7cm long and 2cm across. They are blunt-ended with several bumps. The seeds are oval and slightly angular.

The species is confined in the wild to Tobi Shima, a small island off the west coast of Honshu, Japan. A sample was sent to New York by T. Susa and in 1930 it bloomed there for the first time. In 1964 Kitamura suggested the plant was a variety

Figure 13 *Hemerocallis exaltata*.

of *H. dumortieri*, whereas Stout was inclined to attribute it to *H. middendorffii*. Furthermore the species seems to be somewhat variable, because on a visit to Tobi Shima in 1970 Matsuoka found several variants. Among these were some that bloomed only in the afternoon and some in which the flowers were arranged wreath-like. I have one of these in my garden and although it is worth having, it grows but slowly.

Synonyms: *H. exilis* (Satake 1947) = *nomen erratum*, since plants of this type do not exist.

H. flava (Linnaeus 1762) = synonym for *H. lilioasphodelus* Linnaeus emend. Hylander.

H. forrestii (Diels 1912)

The strong mid-green foliage grows to about 30cm long and the soil around the plant is constantly covered with leaves that have died off. The outer leaves are bent back, whereas the inner ones grow erect. The scape rises from the outer foliage, is 30–40cm long and branches repeatedly at the end. It has small bracts 1cm long as well as some 6cm in length.

The five to eight, sometimes even ten, orange-red blooms are set on pedicels 2–3cm long. The flowers are funnel-shaped with tubes 1.2–2cm in length. The segments of the flower are 3–4cm wide; they are not veined and the midrib is flat. The longish, flat-ended seed capsules are 3.5cm long with a diameter of 2cm.

The species grows on dry ridges and rocky banks in the north-west of Yunnan at altitudes of around 250m. There are two distinct kinds, one

Figure 14 *Hemerocallis forrestii*.

with red-orange flowers and one with pure orange ones, but neither contains the fulvous dye. The former corresponds with the original description of the species, discovered by Forrest in 1906. Even in a cold greenhouse *H. forrestii* will die back during the winter, while it is unlikely to survive in Europe out in the open.

Plants labelled *H. forrestii* 'Perry's Variety', which are grown in some botanical gardens, are not a winter-hardy clone but a hybrid from *H. forrestii* × *H. middendorffii*, produced by Amos Perry in 1946.

H. fulva (Linnaeus 1762)

The roots, with their spindle-shaped swellings and their ability to spread, find the edging to a flower bed no obstacle. The leaves are folded in a 'V' shape and are up to 90cm long by up to 3cm wide. While the outer leaves are arched, the inner ones are erect. The scapes overtop the foliage and are branched in the upper quarter of their length. The bracts are lanceolate.

The colour of the blooms varies greatly from a rusty-orange through red and rosy-pink to a sort of combination of all these colours. In our gardens the plants of this kind originate mainly from the clone 'Europa' (see below). The tube is 2–3cm long; the segments are reflexed and wavy along the edge, and the veins, which are conspicuous, branch near the edge. The elliptical seed capsules are 3cm in length, blunt and indented at the end. The seeds are egg-shaped.

H. fulva is common and widespread in the wild. There are various clones and these are presumably local variations, as Wildenow discovered as early as 1799, when he observed several kinds in Germany alone, some small, some big, several with fulvous blooms and others paler. It is thanks to the work of J. Schabell (USA) and R.M. Kitchingman (UK) that there is now some sort of order among the varieties and clones.

Several of these are self-sterile with a triploid chromosome complement. However, Stout also noticed several self-fertile forms. The various clones and varieties are listed below.

'Chengtu' This was selected by Stout in 1935 from plants sent from Chengtu to New York by Professor Fang. The orange flowers have a scarlet edge. The foliage remains green until the first frost.

'Cypriani' This was sent to Charles Sprenger by Father Cypriani, who was a missionary in Hupeh, China. The blooms are a coppery-red with golden centres; the segments of the perianth glisten and each has a golden median stripe. The scape stands 1m tall.

'Europa' This is the most widely grown sort, with flowers of a typical fulvous-red colour, broad eye-zone and clearly visible veins of a darker colour. It is interesting to note that, although it is self-sterile, since it is triploid, its pollen is fertile. This is why it became the male parent

Figure 15 *Hemerocallis fulva*.

of many of the early hybrids and assumed importance in the development of modern plants. It grows long stolons and every piece of root is capable of regenerating itself into a new plant. It has no difficulty in establishing itself in a lawn and I have even seen it growing through tarmac.

'Festival' This is a clone selected by Stout. It has red-brown flowers, an orange throat and a similar median stripe. The outer segments are reflexed, the inner ones slightly concave and the overall diameter of the flower is 7.5cm.

'Flore Pleno' Although the flowers are double, this clone is in no way identical to 'Kwanzo'; despite this, it is often sold in the UK as such! This is the plant Veitch described as *H. fulva disticha flora pleno*. He received it some time before 1860 from Rev. Ellis from China. The 15cm orange flowers have the outer segments (sepals) widely curved back. The red eye-zone is more conspicuous than in 'Kwanzo'.

'Hankow' This has flowers 13cm across. The colour is a more yellowy-orange, with purple to scarlet eye. Stout received his specimen from the American Consul in Hankow, a town in the province of Hupeh in China, and in 1939 Farr introduced it into the trade.

'Hupehensis' The place of origin of this clone is very similar to the last, but the flowers in this case are copper-red with a yellow throat and wavy edges. It was sent to Charles Sprenger by Father Cypriani and was described in *The Gardeners' Chronicle* in 1916.

'Kwanzo' ('Kwanso') The roots of this form appear somewhat enlarged; the foliage is green and grows to as much as 90cm long, as does the strong erect scape. This is multi-branched and the membranous bracts are roughly ovate-acuminate. The blooms are double and the colour is more like that of the 'Europa' clone, that is to say that they are a fulvous-red with darker eyes. Moreover, unlike 'Flore Pleno', it comes from Japan, where it grows in Hokkaido, Honshu, Shikoku and Kyushi. Its name there is 'Quanso', a corruption of the Chinese 'Hsuan Tsao'. We find the first mention of it in 1712 in Kaempfer's *Amoenitatum Exoticarum*, which was a report of his residence in Japan from 1690 to 1692 as an officer of the Dutch East India Company. This form is triploid and sterile.

'Kwanzo Variegata' The flowers resemble those of the previous clone, but the foliage is variegated, i.e. striped white and green. Of the two forms, this was the first to arrive in Europe and to be called 'Kwanzo'. In 1784 Thunberg wrote a description of it in *Flora Japonica* and it was again described in 1864 in *The Gardeners' Chronicle*.

'Margaret Perry' This was selected by Amos Perry from some seedlings of a cross between 'Europa' and 'Cypriani'. The orange-red flowers have a cadmium-red (orange to bright red) median stripe.

'Red Bird' This variety was selected from 'Chengtu' seedlings.

The orange flowers have strongly marked red throats and bright yellow midribs.

'Speciosa' This was registered in 1937 by R. Wallace of Colchester, having been selected from some of Amos Perry's seedlings. It was described as flowering late with radiant red blooms.

'Theron' This was selected by Stout and is a lovely dark red clone with a scape of 70cm.

'Vieux Carré' This clone was taken by some early migrants from Europe to America and is common in Louisiana and other southern states. It is evergreen, blooms very late and has a pronounced halo (see p. 63).

Synonym: *H. crocea* (Lamarck 1799).

H. fulva var. *angustifolia*
(Baker 1871)

This is a small plant with a scape only 30cm long, but leaves of 30–40cm. The small orange flowers consist of narrow pointed segments and have red halos. A relationship with *H. fulva* is unlikely and the plant is probably closer to the *nana* group. This variety is not grown in Europe.

Baker based his description of the plant on dry material that came from northern India. Unfortunately he confused the issue somewhat by regarding *H. fulva* var. *longituba* from Japan as a synonym of this species without ever having inspected any specimens of the latter plant. Because of the great distances between their habitats, his conclusion is most improbable. On the other hand, the flora of western Yunan, where *H.*

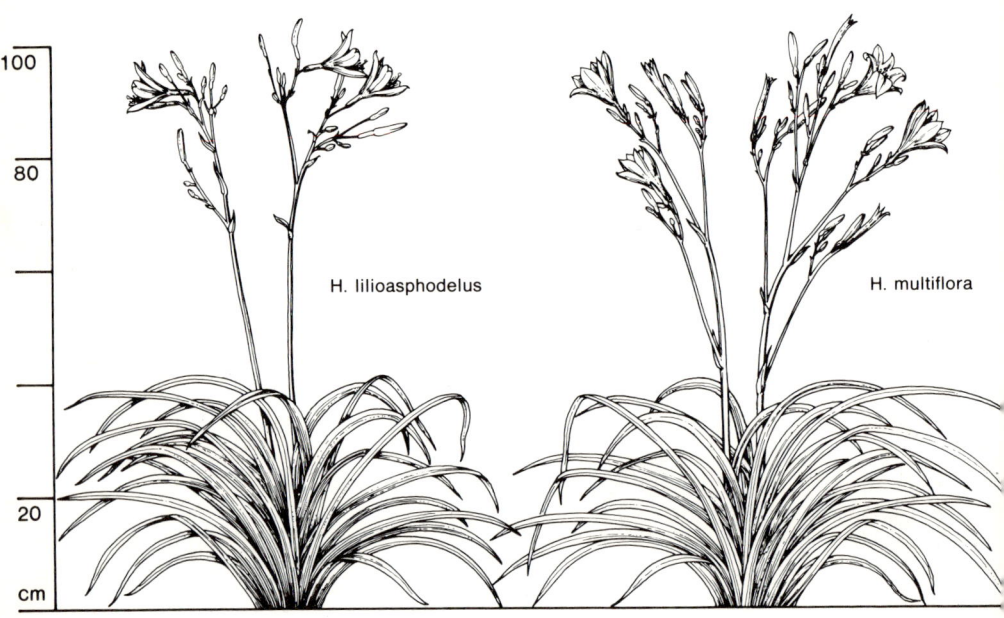

Figure 16 Growth habits and comparative sizes of *Hemerocallis* species (2).

forrestii and *H. nana* grow, is closely related to the flora of India.

H. fulva var. *disticha* (Baker 1874)

This plant has smooth, shiny leaves 90cm long. The scape of 60–90cm emerges from one side of the leaf fan and branches several times. The leaf-like bracts are between 2 and 4cm long. At each junction of the branches are six bell-shaped flowers with tubes of 4cm. The latter are of a pale yellow colour, whereas the rest of the flower is a reddish-orange with pure orange median stripes and also an orange-coloured throat. The segments have veins, which branch near the edge, and their shape is lanceolate running to a slender point, reflexed and wavy along the edge.

There was a shipment of these day lilies in 1789 from Macao in southern China to Great Britain and this was distributed among several botanical gardens. It also became available for purchase, but it was soon apparent that, although the plant grew well in the open, it failed to flower. This is not surprising when one considers that it is used to a sub-tropical climate; given the right conditions it blooms profusely.

Synonym: *H. disticha* (Donahue et David 1825).

H. fulva var. *littorea* [(Makino) Matsuoka et Hotta 1964]

The extensive roots of the plant are spindle-shaped and of a light yellow colour. The dark green leaves are

85cm long and 2cm wide with prominent veins. The scape branches at the tip and has numerous proliferations. The upper bracts are a sort of oval to elongated triangular shape, but the lower ones are lanceolate and about 5cm long. The number of blooms can vary considerably.

The flowers are set on stalks 10cm long and are a dark orange-red, or orange-yellow. The tube is up to 3cm long and the free parts of the segments spread wide to a diameter of 7.5cm. The inner segments (petals) are lanceolate and reflexed, displaying a dark brown eye-zone and light midribs. The 3cm long seed capsules are conspicuously ribbed.

This variety grows not far from the sea in Kanto in the Japanese district of Honshu, which is why it is sometimes also called 'Coastal Day Lily'. Its flowers vary in colour and in size.

As long ago as 1941, Stout suspected that the plants that he had received from Nakai in Japan were probably a variety of *H. fulva*. In 1964 Matsuoka and Hotta also ascribed them to this species, which is supported by plants now growing in the USA.

Synonyms: *H. littorea* (Makino 1924)

H. aurantiaca var. *littorea* (Nakai 1932).

H. fulva var. *longituba* (Maximowicz 1885)

The crown of this plant is always obscured by the fibrous remains of its old, dead leaves. The 1m long scape branches only near its apex and the elliptical bracts are 1–2cm long. The orange-yellow flowers have a fulvous flush. The tube is long and narrow.

This variety is indigenous to certain regions of Japan. Some Japanese botanists, such as Nakai and Ohwi, have suggested that var. *longituba* might be a separate species, but the Japanese fulva species have much in common with the Chinese, as is shown by the degree of morphological agreement. In 1949 Ohwi mentioned a plant called *H. sendaica*; he corrected himself in 1965 when he conceded that this was a synonym for *H. fulva* var. *longituba*.

Synonym: *H. longituba* (Miquel 1867).

H. fulva var. *maculata* (Baroni 1897)

This variety grows very strongly, having light green foliage with leaves up to 130cm long and 3cm wide. Since the upper quarter of the leaf is bent downwards, the scape at 120cm

Figure 17   *Hemerocallis fulva* var. *littorea*.

still manages to overtop the foliage. It branches between two and four times, carrying eight to twelve flowers on stalks 1cm long. The bracts are up to 7cm in length. The cup-shaped flowers are golden-yellow with a cadmium-yellow throat that leads to a tube 4cm long. It has a pronounced purple-red eye and yellow median stripes. The points of the 15cm flower are curled back; they look waxy and glisten.

H. fulva var. *maculata* comes from Shenshi in China; Giraldi found it there in 1895 and sent it to Baroni in Florence. Because the variety is triploid it reproduces vegetatively, but the pollen is fertile and so can be used for breeding. Stout crossed the variety with *H. citrina* among others.

H. fulva var. pauciflora (Hotta et Matsuoka 1966)

The leaves of this plant grow 20–30cm long. There are few branches on the scape, which carries no more than one, two, or possibly three flowers. In Europe and America it hardly ever flowers, even if, as Dr Hu tried in 1969, it is potted.

It was discovered on Honshu, Japan at an altitude of about 180m. *H. fulva* var. *pauciflora* together with *H. fulva* 'Europa' and 'Kwanzo' and var. *maculata* brings the number of known triploids of the *Hemerocallis* genus to four.

H. fulva var. rosea (Stout 1930)

The scape extends well above the narrow, dark green foliage. The 10cm flowers are rosy-red and have greenish-yellow tubes 2.5cm long. The free ends of the segments are curled back widely, displaying a distinctive purple eye-zone and light orange median stripe. The edges of the segments are wavy.

The variety is a native of Kuling, which is part of the province of Kiang-shi in China. Dr A.N. Steward discovered the plant there and sent a sample to Stout. In the course of more botanical expeditions Dr Steward found additional clones of this variety, 'Rosalind' with an eye-zone and 'Pastel rose' without. Elizabeth Nesmith of Kew Gardens also received a clone without an eye, which she used to produce a number of different hybrids. Amos Perry used this variety to create a good red strain and he eventually registered 36 of them, but they are no longer obtainable. In 1954 Traub treated 'Rosalind' with colchicine and in this way developed one of the first ever tetraploid types.

H. fulva var. sempervirens (Hotta et Matsuoka 1966)

I have a plant of this variety in my garden, but as yet it has been reluctant to flower. Therefore the following description is based on information from John Schabell and Dr Thomas Barr, who obtained their seeds, just as I did, from Dr Shuichi Hirao in Japan. The flower is a strong fulvous colour with an orange lustre; there is an obvious red-brown eye. Earlier references give it four to six blooms per scape. However, this is something of an understatement, as proved by a report from Thomas Barr in which he writes of 104 buds on scapes 125cm long!

He is also of the opinion that the plant is in no way a variety of *H.*

fulva, but rather a local type of *H. aurantiaca*, or a variety of it. He supports his argument by pointing out that varieties of both these cross well with one another, whereas each is almost as self-sterile as the other. At this point I would simply like to add that the proposition supports my theory that *H. fulva* and *H. aurantiaca* form one group. The home of *H. fulva* var. *sempervirens* is on Amami Ooshima, a small island south of Okinawa.

Claims relating to the flowering period also require close examination. In Japan the plant is called 'Akino Wasure Gisa', which means something like 'the flowers come when you no longer think about them'. In the USA it blooms from the end of July to the onset of frost, but in Europe it might well begin flowering later.

Synonym: *H. sempervirens* (Araki 1952).

H. graminea (Andrews 1802)

The leaves of this compact plant grow up to 75cm long; they are straight and have a grass-like keel. In contrast to this the scape, which is much the same length, is a little arched and carries two to three flowers. The 5cm long bracts are lanceolate in shape and turn brown immediately after flowering.

The green buds have a brownish tinge. Once the bud has opened, the flower will last two to three days. With a diameter of 12cm the flowers are relatively big; the tube is short and the inner segments (petals) are 2.5cm wide. The flower is a strong orange colour with a yellow throat. The flower segments have wavy

Figure 18 *Hemerocallis graminea.*

edges and are brown on the outside.

From Maximowicz's notes we learn that the species is a native of Siberia. In his report on the flora of the River Amur region he tells us about two forms of the small-leaved *Hemerocallis*. The one with the longer scape and longer tube he named *H. graminea* and the other *H. graminea* f. *humilior*. It is the latter that is described here. Its habitat stretches from the upper Amur region as far as Lake Baikal. The original *H. graminea*, on the other hand, is now designated as *H. minor* and has a more southerly habitat, from the lower course of the Amur to the River Ussuri. In 1930 Bailey made the first clear distinction between the two kinds.

The relationship between the two should thus have been firmly established, had Stout not received quite a different form of *H. graminea* in 1926, which he then described as a dwarf form of *H. dumortieri*. In Europe we have to date no certified specimen that might allow us to resolve the problem.

H. hakunensis (Nakai 1943)

The narrow-keeled leaves are from 60 to 75cm long. The branched scape, 85–100cm in length, reaches above them and bears from six to eleven flowers. The oval bracts are from 1.2 to 3cm long.

The orange blooms have tubes of 2–2.5cm in length. The flower segments, with a length of up to 7.5cm, are thus fairly long, compared with their relatively slender width of only 1.2–1.5cm. The seed capsules are a broad-elliptical shape with three upright lobes on the upper surface that are fissured horizontally. These lobed seed capsules provide a way of differentiating this plant from *H. esculenta*, to which this species is closely related. It grows in the region of Mount Tusan in South Korea.

H. × hippeastroides (Sprenger 1908)

A putative hybrid by Willy Müller, said to have originated from *H. minor crocea* × *H. thunbergii*. However, the plant got lost in Willy Müller's nursery, the 'Hortus Nucerensis'.

H. lilioasphodelus (Linnaeus emend. Hylander 1753)

The strong tufts of foliage have leaves 75cm long that are widely spread so as to give the plant a large diameter. The fibrous roots swell here and there to form spindle-shaped storage organs. The thin stiff scape reaches well above the foliage and branches in the upper quarter of its height. The lanceolate bracts are 4cm long.

The beautiful lemon-yellow blooms are borne on short stalks 3mm long. The flowers open at night and last between 20 and 76 hours! The cylindrical tube is approximately

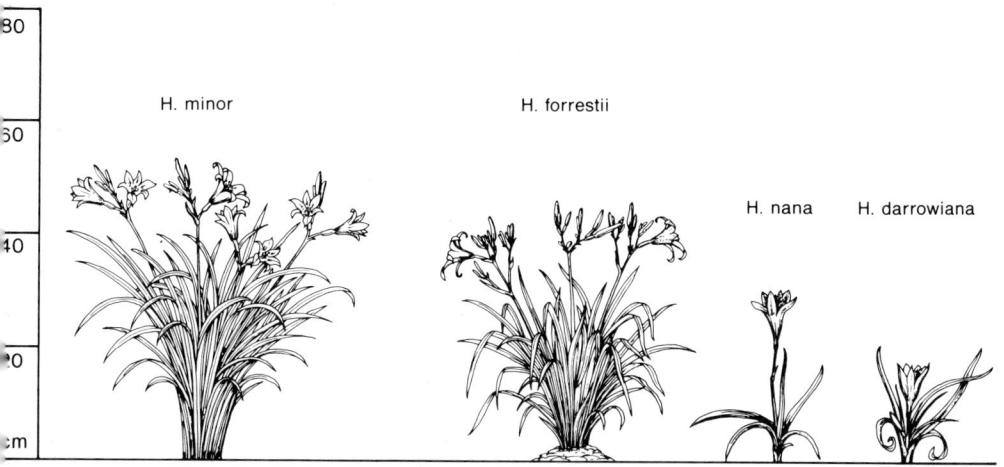

Figure 19 Growth habits and comparative sizes of *Hemerocallis* species (3).

2.5cm long and the mouth of the flower from 7.5 to 10cm in diameter, with the segments overlapping each other. The seed capsules are oval to elliptical, often covered with warts and look wrinkled when ripe. The seeds themselves are almost round.

This was one of the earliest day lilies used for breeding, and descendants of this plant have inherited many excellent characteristics. *H. lilioasphodelus* is fairly tolerant of wet soils and has long-lasting flowers that are fragrant. In 1928 Morrison mentioned a specially selected clone notable for its strong scent, but it has not been distinguished by name. The name *H. flava* is still in use occasionally, but is not botanically correct.

Synonyms: *H. flava* (Linnaeus 1762), *H. lutea* (Gaertner 1790).

H. littorea (Makino 1924)
= Synonym for *H. fulva* var. *littorea* [(Makino) Matsuoka et Hotta 1964].

H. longituba (Miquel 1867)
= Synonym for *H. fulva* var. *longituba* (Maximowicz 1885).

H. lutea (Gaertner 1790)
= Synonym for *H. lilioasphodelus* (Linnaeus emend. Hylander 1753).

H. × *luteola* (Jenkins 1900)
= Hybrid from *H. aurantiaca* 'Major' × *H. thunbergii*, which was described in detail by Mallet in 1903, as well as by Stout in 1930. The latter also published an illustration of this plant. It has golden-yellow trumpet-shaped flowers about 15cm across.

H. micrantha (Nakai 1943)
The leaves are dark green and can grow to a length of 80cm and a width of 3cm. The scape is much taller than the foliage and it branches at the tip; nevertheless it carries only four blooms. The upper bracts are more of an oval shape as compared with the lower ones, which are lanceolate and grow up to 7.5cm long. The orange flowers have tubes 2cm long and noticeably narrow segments that are blunt-ended. The latter grow to 3.5cm long by 6mm wide.

Figure 20 *Hemerocallis lilioasphodelus*.

Figure 21 *Hemerocallis × luteola.*

Figure 22 *Hemerocallis middendorffii.*

Nakai found this species near Tyosen and Keinan in Korea. Dr Hu suspects that it is closely related to *H. multiflora* and *H. plicata*.

H. middendorffii (*Trautvetter et Meyer 1856*)

This species produces an abundance of flat, smooth foliage. The leaves are 1.5cm wide and are bent over at the top. The fibrous roots are cylindrical and do not extend far. The unbranched scape grows erect to a height of 90cm. The bracts are broadly oval, almost a mussel shape, and overlap at the base. Occasionally they may suddenly become narrower towards their free end and when this occurs the edge is thin and colourless.

The intensely orange flowers are of a clear glowing colour and almost odourless. They are dish-shaped, with a diameter of 7.5cm and a tube of only 12mm. The 5.5cm long sepals are elliptical, whereas the petals are 1cm longer and spatulate in shape. When the flower is fully open the points are bent back. The broadly elliptical seed capsules grow to 3cm and are distinctly grooved.

Its habitat is the lower Amur basin, as well as Sakhalin Island and the island of Hokkaido in Japan. A.T. von Middendorff collected the first specimens of this species in the Amur region and it was later described at the Botanical Garden of St. Petersburg. The species is somewhat variable and some forms occur with slight branching about 3cm below the inflorescence. The length of the flower stalk and the colour of the flower also vary. These morphological differences were corroborated in 1944 by Kawano, who carried out a chromosome study of the species and found several caryotypes during his investigations.

The species has played a considerable role in the development of modern hybrids. One of the plant's disadvantages is that it does not 'clean' itself, i.e. the flowers do not fall off by themselves when they have finished blooming. On the other hand a point very much in their favour is that the plants can be relied upon to bloom for a second time in September.

H. minor (Miller 1768)

The plant is of low and compact growth, the flowers held high above the foliage. The string-like roots sometimes have bulbous swellings at their tips. The leaves, which grow to a length of 55cm, lean slightly backwards and are only 6–8mm wide. The slender scape is between 45 and 60cm high; it branches at its tip and carries two to three, sometimes five, flowers.

These flowers are more or less bell-shaped, with a 2cm long tube. The 3cm long segments are a strong chrome or cadmium-yellow and they are fragrant. *H. minor* has long-lasting flowers that, opening on the evening of the first day, do not close again until the third day. The elliptical seed capsule grows to 3cm long and has a diameter of 1.2–1.5cm. The seeds themselves are elliptical rather than round.

The species is native to the steppe-

Figure 23 *Hemerocallis minor*.

lands of northern China, Mongolia, eastern Siberia and Korea. The only problems now are, firstly, whether what Miller described was in fact *H. minor* and, secondly, that in the meantime various other day lilies seem also to have been included under the umbrella of this name. The original plant is closely related to *H. lilioasphodelus*; both, for example, have long-lasting flowers. The Japanese name for the species is 'Matsu-yoi-gusa', which means 'the bush that waits until the evening'.

H. × mülleri (Sprenger 1903)

= Hybrid from *H. thunbergii* × *H. citrina* with very large, scented and long-lasting yellow flowers.

H. multiflora (Stout 1929)

This is a species that flowers profusely. Its leaves are 75cm long, but their ends droop, so that the general height of the foliage is only 45cm. The foliage is very wiry and turns reddish-brown in the autumn. The scape, which grows to a height of 100cm, stands erect at first, but eventually bends under the weight of the flowers and seeds. It branches repeatedly above the halfway point and carries between 75 and 100 blooms! These are orange or cadmium-yellow and are set on pedicels 8–12mm long. The tube is 12mm in length and the flower itself has a diameter of 7.5cm. The sepals are 2.5cm long and the petals somewhat longer; they are sharply reflexed and glisten in strong sunlight. The oval seed capsules are not very big and the seeds are egg-shaped.

The plants come from the province of Honan in China. In 1925 Steward sent some specimens to the New York Botanical Gardens, where Stout later classified them. The species is closely related to *H. micrantha* and *H. plicata*. In China it is not uncommon to find the species growing in peasants' gardens.

Figure 24 *Hemerocallis multiflora.*

H. nana (Smith et Forrest 1916)

This is also a dwarf species with a compact habit of growth. The string-like roots have at their ends club-shaped or spindle-shaped swellings. The sword-shaped leaves are 35cm long and 1cm wide. The scape, which stands only 25cm high, does not branch, but it does have bracts. These are leaf-like and grow 2.5–6cm below the single flower.

The flower is reddish-orange with brown on the outside. The tube is less than 2cm long. The narrow, splayed-out segments give the flower a spidery appearance. The 9mm wide sepals are lanceolate and the petals at 12mm are only marginally wider.

The species grows in the mountains of western Yunan Province in China. In 1913 Forrest discovered it growing in the Yangtse valley up to an altitude of 3000m. In 1939 it was also found at the foot of the snow-

Figure 25 *Hemerocallis nana*.

capped Haba Mountains in sparse pinewoods. It has not, however, shown itself to be winter-hardy either in America or Europe. This is a characteristic it shares with *H. forrestii*, to which it is closely related both morphologically and phytogeographically. The two species, however, differ in the number of blooms they produce.

H. × *ochroleuca (Sprenger 1903)*
(H. thunbergii × *H. citrina)*
This is a hybrid with sulphur-yellow flowers. Although Sprenger praised the extended florescence, in hot weather the flowers tend to close by the following noon, as the plants growing in the Weihenstephan Trial Gardens in Munich prove.

H. pedicellata (Nakai 1932)
The leaves of this species grow to 90cm long and between 1cm and 1.8cm wide. The scape is 65cm long and has a diameter of 8mm. The lanceolate bracts are membranous and between 2 and 3cm long. The orange-red blooms sit on pedicels 3cm long and have tubes measuring 2.5cm. The lanceolate flower segments are 9cm in length.

Despite the detailed measurements given by Nakai this plant is known solely from the specimens collected by Hara on Sakhalin Island. The political situation there is still such as to preclude any further detailed investigation of the species for the time being.

H. plicata (Stapf 1923)
The string-like roots have spindle-shaped swellings near their ends. The leaves are 10–40cm long and folded. The irregularly branched scape can vary in height from 25cm to 55cm and may produce between five and eleven flowers. The pedicels are at most 2cm in length, and the elongated-oval bracts are the same length. The trumpet-shaped flowers are orange-yellow, with a 15mm tube and 7cm long segments. The seed capsules are only 2cm long and thinnish, narrower at the base. Their tops are indented.

The species comes from sub-alpine woods and alpine meadows in the south-west and west of China up as far as the northerly province of

THE SPECIES

Figure 26 *Hemerocallis plicata*.

H. serotina (Focke 1889)
Nomen illegitimum, since it does not differ from *H. thunbergii*.

H. sulphurea (Nakai 1932)
Nomen illegitimum, since it does not differ from *H. thunbergii*.

H. thunbergii (Barr emend. Baker 1890)
These compact plants increase by means of runners. The dark green leaves form a mound 85cm high, but the foliage is graceful because the leaves are only between 0.8 and 2.4cm wide and bent over at the tip. The scape is slender, but never-

Khasia in India. A. Henry and G. Forrest collected the first specimens in Yunnan. *H. plicata* is closely related to *H. multiflora*, differing from the latter not only in height and the number of flowers, but also in the folding of the leaves. It should be noted, however, that this characteristic can disappear if the soil is rich.

H. rutilans (Perry 1924)
Described as a variant of *H. dumortieri* by Amos Perry, but in view of its small, well-formed golden-yellow flowers probably, in fact, a hybrid of *H. dumortieri*.

Figure 27 *Hemerocallis thunbergii*.

theless stands erect to a height of 100–115cm; it branches in the upper quarter and carries from four to as many as 20 flowers. The elongated bracts are lanceolate and broaden out towards the base; the lower ones can grow to as long as 8cm.

The flowers open at night, are fragrant and lemon-yellow with a greenish throat. They are borne on pedicels 1.2–1.8cm long and have tubes up to 3cm in length. The ovate sepals have blunt ends, whereas the petals are spatulate with indented ends. The obovate seed capsules are about 3cm long, with a diameter of 2cm; they narrow abruptly towards the base. The seeds are about 6mm long and elliptical.

The species comes from northern China and Japan, but has also long adorned the gardens of Europe and America. In 1930 Bailey suggested that, by virtue of the priority rule, the species should really be called *H. serotina*, because it had been given that name a year prior to 1890. However, there was evidence that as early as 1873 it had been described under the name *H. thunbergii* by Barr, if only briefly. Apart from *H. sulphurea*, Dr Hu compared *H. vespertina* with *H. thunbergii* and in both instances came to the conclusion that the plants were identical and thus both names were superfluous. More recent research classes *H. vespertina* as a variety of *H. citrina*; this emphasises once again the close interrelationship between the nocturnal-blooming species.

The flowers of *H. thunbergii* remain open for a long time and are fragrant. For this reason the species has been much used for breeding. It also readily produces abundant seed. The best time for pollination is five to eight hours after the flowers have opened, i.e. usually at night.

Synonyms: *H. serotina* (Focke 1889); *H. sulphurea* (Nakai 1932).

H. vespertina (Hara 1941)
Synonym for *H. citrina* var. *vespertina*. For a long time it was thought to be identical with *H. thunbergii* and so was considered a *nomen illegitimum*.

H. × vomerensis (Sprenger 1903)
= Hybrid from *H. thunbergii* × *H. minor* producing yellowish-orange flowers and grass-like foliage.

H. washingtoniana (Traub 1951)
One of the first tetraploid day lilies developed by colchicine treatment. It was given the status of species although this is plainly not permissible.

H. yezoensis (Hara 1937)
The cord-like roots of the plant are fairly thick. The leaves are 2cm wide and grow to a length of 75cm; they stand mainly erect, but are bent over at the end. The 85cm scape carries between four and twelve blooms. The lower bracts are lanceolate, 6cm long; the upper ones more of an oval shape.

The lemon-yellow flowers have only a faint smell; the diameter is between 7 and 10cm and the tube 2–3cm long, usually a greenish-yellow, but sometimes even a purplish-brown. The flower segments grow to a length of 8cm; the lanceolate sepals are 2cm wide and the ovate petals

3cm. The longish seed capsule holds round seeds.

The species grows extensively on the island of Hokkaido, Japan. In the course of his chromosome investigations in 1961, Kawano discovered two caryotypes that can be put down to various causes. Botanists are still not agreed whether the species is more closely related to *H. thunbergii* or *H. lilioasphodelus*. What is certain, however, is that it clearly belongs to this group. In the light of experience gained in the USA it would seem worth growing the plant in Europe.

The introduction of *Hemerocallis* species.

Species	Year	Origin	Introduced by
H. altissima	about 1930	Kiang-shu, China	Steward
H. aurantiaca	about 1870	South China	–
H. citrina	1895	Shen-shi, China	Giraldi
H. coreana	1929	Korea	Dorsett & Morse
H. dumortieri	about 1830	Japan	Siebold
H. esculenta	about 1935	Japan	Nakai
H. exaltata	about 1930	Tobi Shima, Jap.	Susa
H. forrestii	1906	Yunnan, China	Forrest
H. fulva	before 1576	China	–
var. *littorea*	about 1941	Japan	Nakai
var. *longituba*	about 1930	China	Steward
var. *maculata*	about 1895	Shen-shi, China	Giraldi
var. *rosea*	about 1924	Kiang-shi, China	Steward
'Kwanzo'	about 1860	Japan	Maximowicz?
H. graminea	before 1795	upper Amur reg.	–
H. lilioasphodelus	before 1576	China	–
H. middendorffii	1860	lower Amur reg.	Maximowicz
H. minor	about 1748	eastern Siberia	Gmelin
H. multiflora	1925	Hunan, China	Steward
H. nana	–	Yunnan, China	Forrest
H. plicata	1916	Yunnan, China	Forrest
H. thunbergii	about 1873	–	Kew Gardens

MODERN HYBRIDS

Colours and Patterns

Colour Variations

The wild species of day lily have flowers in a very limited range of colours: yellows, oranges and fulvous-brown. By comparison the modern hybrid day lilies have flowers in almost every colour of the rainbow, lacking only true blue and pure white. It is therefore hardly surprising that nine out of ten *Hemerocallis* growers go for cultivars and even occasionally experiment with hybridising programmes of their own. Without listing all the intermediate tones, or colours tinged or flushed with other colours, there is at present a choice of 16 different colours:

- near-white
- light yellow
- strong yellow
- orange
- copper
- peach or melon
- flesh tones (light tones)
- brown
- rose-pink
- rose-red
- pale red
- deep red
- dark mahogany red (almost black)
- lavender
- purple
- almost blue.

The colours may not always be solid and may vary in the ways mentioned below.

Dusting and Dotting

Diamond Dusting This is a phenomenon whereby the day lily blooms glisten and sparkle in the sun as if dusted with silver or as if hundreds of tiny diamonds had been sprinkled over them. The effect is brought about by a superfluity of dye-enhancing agents, which are themselves colourless, belonging to a group of organic chemicals called flavonoids. There is also an effect known as 'gold dusting', which is much the same except that it is golden instead of silvery. It can occur with strong orange or red types. It is a great pity that one cannot capture these effects with a camera; it is something that one has to see for oneself.

Dotting This, on the other hand, can be captured with a camera. This phenomenon makes it look as if the base colour has been dusted over with another colour. The flowers are dotted with spots of colour, the spots varying in size from that of a speck of dust to a freckle. Thus, not only are there the 16 plain colours mentioned above, but there are also three overlays, i.e. four possibilities:

   plain colour
   dotting
   diamond dusting
   gold dusting.

Colour Distribution

The flowers of day lilies may be:

   self-coloured
   blended
   polychrome
   bitone
   reverse bitone
   bicolour
   reverse bicolour.

Self colour means that the sepals and petals are alike in colour and shading. This does not mean, however, that the bloom cannot also have a throat of another colour. (Throat shape and colour are further discussed below.)

A flower is called **blended** when it has two different colours, but these are distributed evenly on both sets of tepals. Thus a flower that is a blend of pink and yellow has sepals and petals in these colours and not petals of one colour and sepals of the other.

Polychrome describes a flower displaying more than two colours evenly spread over the whole. 'Little Rainbow', for example, is such a mixture, consisting of melon, pink and yellow. If you add to this a contrasting throat as well as the colour of the anthers, this normally pastel-coloured type can, in fact, become quite colourful without being gaudy.

This applies also to **bitone**, as against bicolour. In the former the petals and sepals are alike in colour, but differ in terms of shading and intensity. It is important to note that in each case the petals are always the darker segments. Thus, if the petals are red or a pinkish-red, the sepals might well be rose or pink.

Reverse bitone is when the sepals, the outer segments, are darker than the inner segments, the petals. In other words, as the name implies, it is the reverse of the previous sort.

Bicolour blooms are more dramatic in their colouring. Some have been so gaudy that they have gone out of fashion at present. The petals and the sepals are of completely different colours, for instance, red and yellow, or yellow and lilac. The outer segments have the lighter colour.

Reverse bicolour describes the types where the lighter colour is on the inner segments, i.e. as the name indicates, it is the reverse of the above. Just to recap, bitone and bicolour are two completely different effects. The former has the two colours distributed evenly over both the sepals and the petals, and the latter has petals of one colour and sepals of another.

Patterning

The appearance of a bloom can be much enhanced if there is some kind of coloured marking on it. This is why modern breeders are swinging

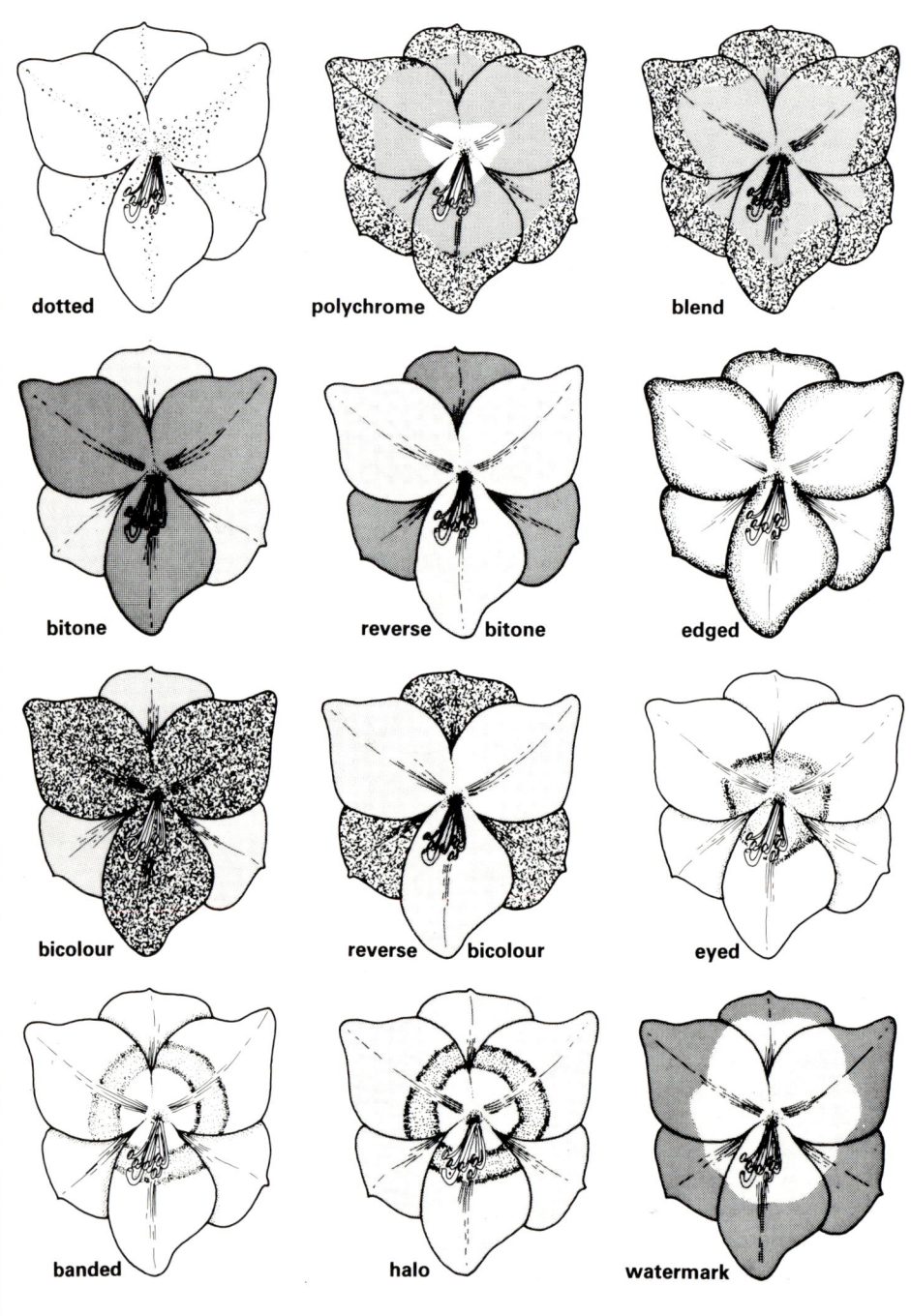

Figure 28 Colour patterning of *Hemerocallis* flowers.

away from bicoloured varieties to patterned ones. The patterns on day lily flowers may be categorised as follows:

    simple
    eyed
    banded
    halo
    watermark
    edged
    tipped
    picotee.

'Simple' means that there is no pattern of any kind.

A day lily flower is said to be **eyed** if, apart from a throat colour, the segments have on them another contrasting or strenghtened colour marking. This blotch or stripe stands out from the background colour of the petals and the sepals. The colour of the eye is always stronger or darker, and the feature is very obvious; this is in sharp contrast to a watermark (see below).

A **banded** flower is very similar to an eyed one, but differs in that the second colour shows on the inner tepals but not on the outer ones. The band generally appears further from the centre of the flower.

Occasionally the band is only faintly visible, but usually this occurs only when the band is merely a different tone, rather than a different colour. This phenomenon is called a **halo** and it does not matter whether the halo is darker or lighter than the background tone; either is possible.

The **watermark** is analogous to the halo, in that it is like an eye in another shade of the background colour. Usually it appears as a slightly lighter tone of the background colour, so that one often has to look twice because one thinks that the flower may have faded. This is a feature that may well escape the casual observer entirely.

A more recent innovation in plant breeding is the **edged** flower. This is a comparatively rare trait, although there are some striking examples, such as 'Ann Blocher' (1980), which has bright pink flowers with a strong lilac-pink edge to the segments. It is also possible to get a dark flower with a very light, almost white edge. One should beware of confusing this effect with genuine fading, which happens to some flowers when subjected to intense sunshine.

Tipped describes those types where the edging effect is confined to the ends of the petals. The area of edging should not exceed one-third of the diameter of the flower, otherwise one cannot tell the difference between this phenomenon and an eye. It is immaterial whether the tipped effect manifests itself as another colour or is simply tonal.

Picotee effect describes the narrow line of contrasting colour round the edges of the sepals and petals. 'Chicago Picotee Memories' is a good example of this.

Throat Colour

The colour of the throat can also vary. There are three basic colour possibilities and various intermediate shades. The size of the throat is also important and may be categorised as small, large or dilated, the latter being those in which the colour stretches out finger-like on to the petals. The three basic colours for the throat are:

yellow
orange
green,

and the sizes:

small
large
dilated.

The colour of the throat can influence the overall appearance of the flower. A yellow throat, for example, does not contrast as sharply with a red flower as does a green one. On the other hand the latter goes better with a light yellow flower and a strong yellow flower profits from an orange throat. If breeders wish to improve their plants, they need to attend to details like these. Even when there is total uniformity of colour, the throat is still a factor to bear in mind, even though in this instance its colour is the same as the rest of the flower.

Anthers

The colour of the anthers can vary and without suggesting that this can make a radical difference to the overall appearance of a flower, it does have some effect. It makes a difference whether the anthers contrast with or are of the same colour as the flower. Anthers may be yellow or orange, or they may be grey or near-black tinged with lilac or a reddish hue. The variations increase the total number of possible flower forms available.

Midribs or Median Stripes

A median stripe is a stripe along the middle of a petal or sepal. It may be prominent or flat. In American catalogues this may be described as 'prominent veins'. The presence or absence of median stripes brings another four possibilities:

absent altogether
present on petals only
present on sepals only
present on petals and sepals.

If median stripes do occur they are, more often than not, to be found on the petals and they tend to be more distinct since their colour differs from that of the flower. On the other hand, where they occur on the sepals they are recognisable simply by virtue of a difference in tone. Par-

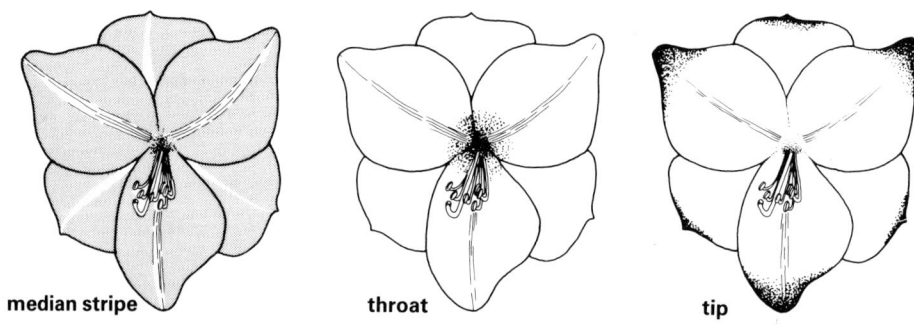

Figure 29 Other designs are created by the colour of the median stripe, the throat and the tips of the segments.

ticularly conspicuous are those median stripes that are not only strongly-coloured, but also have a raised central vein. From the breeding point of view it is very much more difficult to obtain absolutely flat broad median stripes.

Median stripes are usually white, yellow, pink or lavender in colour. In the main, white and yellow stripes tend to go with flowers that are red, purple, golden or melon. With the last named sorts lavender or pink stripes occasionally occur. In light pink flowers not only is the median stripe more strongly coloured, but the veins of the petals are distinct by virtue of their colour.

Flower Shapes

Side View

The shape of a flower may be described as seen from the side or as seen from in front.

The front view tells us something about the geometric shape of the flower, whereas the side view describes the nature of the flower segments. There are six side view possibilities:

> flat
> trumpet
> flaring
> recurved

as well as two types of

> double.

Flat flowers have, as a rule, a small throat from which the segments stretch straight to the edge of the flower. 'Cartwheels' is a flower of this sort and aptly named.

Just as straight are the segments of **trumpet-shaped** flowers, only in this case the angle with the throat is steeper, giving more or less a funnel shape. The mouth is open wide enough to give a glimpse of the interior of the flower.

Flared flowers are those that look as if the segments have been drawn over the edge of a bowl and so arch out uniformly from the throat. A flared side view often goes with a triangular front view.

The perianth segments are said to be **recurved** when their free ends not only arch but are bent back. Since this often happens where the segments are at their broadest, it tends to give them a heavier, spade-shaped appearance.

The term **double** describes those types of day lily flowers that are made up of more than six segments. What happens is that stamens become petal-like, sometimes even with an anther attached. The number of segments, including additional petals, can vary from six or more to 18. A flower with 18 segments looks almost over-full.

There are in fact two types of double day lily flower, the azalea type, also known as *layer-on-layer*, and the paeony type, or *hose-in-hose*. In the latter the extra segments give the flower a powder-puff appearance. If in addition the edges are also ruffled, as they are in 'Betty Woods', the effect can be very pretty. As the name implies, the azalea type of double has one layer of petals lying more or less on top of the other.

Front View

There are six possible variations on the shape of the flower as seen from

MODERN HYBRIDS

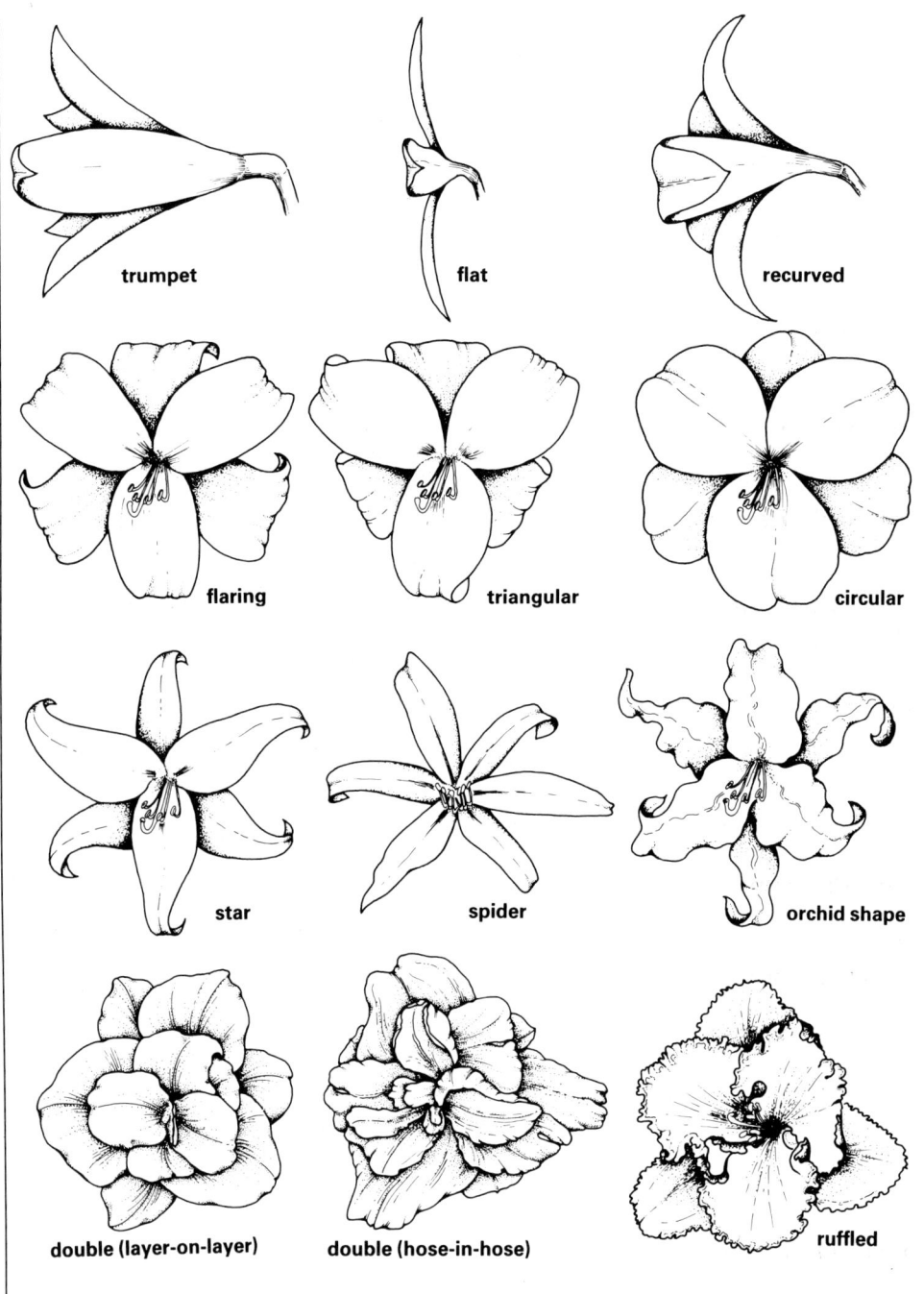

Figure 30 The shapes of *Hemerocallis* flowers.

the front. The six front views are:

- circular
- triangular
- star-shaped
- spider
- orchid-shaped
- informal.

The **circular** shape comes about when the segments, usually short and blunt-ended, overlap, creating a flower that is almost circular in outline. Such a flower is very solid looking, which is particularly effective for the small-flowered varieties.

The **triangular** shape occurs when the petals are recurved and the fold of the petals coincides with the line of the sepals.

A **star-shaped** flower occurs when the segments are unusually long and pointed. In this way a three-pointed star is formed, or, if there is enough room between the inner segments to reveal the outer ones, a six-pointed star.

The **spider** effect is much like a star shape except that the segments are also extraordinarily narrow and so do not overlap.

The term **orchid-shaped** is applied to flowers whose segments are so ragged or twisted as to have a fancied resemblance to certain types of orchid.

When a bloom seems to lack any kind of uniformity the term **informal** is used.

Shape of the Segments

One of the key factors in the general appearance of the flower is the shape of the individual segments. These may be:

- rounded
- pointed
- pinched or twisted.

The term **rounded** is self-explanatory. **Pointed** and **pinched** differ in that a pointed segment is of regular triangular shape, narrowing gradually to a point, whereas pinched means the segment is very broad at the base and suddenly narrows at the tip. The term **twisted** denotes a segment that is twisted along its longitudinal axis, like a propeller, so that at the tip the back is at the front.

Edges

There are three types of edge to day lily flowers:

- tailored
- ribbed
- ruffled.

The word **tailored** more or less speaks for itself; it suggests something beautifully made and impeccably finished. By contrast a recent trend has been to breed day lilies with flowers whose edges are crimped. Such edges are called **ribbed** or **ruffled**. At first there were very few such day lilies and they tended to be much sought after and were correspondingly expensive. Many such varieties are now available. This ruffled effect seems to go particularly well with doubles and circular-shaped flowers, but looks disastrous on triangular or star-shaped flowers.

Texture

A similar rippled or ribbed texture can occur on the surface of the petals and sepals, giving them the appearance of crêpe paper. This effect is often found in varieties raised in the southern states of America. They are often not satisfactory in the UK and Europe, the flowers tending to collapse or develop holes. A smooth-textured flower is generally preferable.

The texture has a considerable influence on how one sees the colour of the flower. A rough surface tends to absorb light and, because it casts shadows, tends to enhance the colour, especially with darker colours. A smooth surface, on the other hand, reflects light and so lends brilliance and luminosity. Sometimes the segments can look as if they are made of wax.

Flower Size

Flower Size
International convention divides day lily flowers into four groups. The measurements are across the face of the flower:

> miniature (less than 7.5cm)
> small (7.5–11.5cm)
> large (11.6–17.5cm)
> giant (greater than 17.5cm).

From an aesthetic point of view the size of the flower should bear some relationship to the length of the scape. A miniature bloom would look ridiculous on a tall scape, as would a giant bloom on a short one.

Flowering Habits

Time of Day
Day lilies do not necessarily bloom just during the day or for one day only, as their name might suggest. With some the flowers open in the evening and develop overnight. A desirable attribute in hybrids is a longer blooming period, and modern hybrids differ from older sorts not only in the beauty and profusion of their flowers, but also, and perhaps more importantly, in their extended flowering period. Day lilies are divided into three groups according to their period of flower:

> diurnal (day blooming)
> extended blooming
> nocturnal (night blooming).

The majority of day lilies are **diurnal**, especially the species and the older varieties. As a rule each flower lasts long enough to allow one to form an opinion as to its worth, even if one is out at work during the day. The duration of the flower should not be so brief that it fades and wilts by mid-afternoon. It is not worthwhile keeping plants of this kind that one has raised oneself.

Nocturnal blooming is invariably a trait inherited from species of the *citrina* group, since all the species in this group have this characteristic. The flowers open in the early evening, remain open throughout the night and wilt in the forenoon or early afternoon. When crossed with day-blooming sorts this can lead to extended blooming. Since members of the *citrina* group are also noted for their fragrance, such crosses often inherit the fragrance, so that the flower is not only pleasing to the eye, but also to the nose.

All **extended** blooming *Hemerocallis* flowers must remain open for at least 16 hours otherwise they cannot aspire to this description. The flower may last from one morning to the next, or from one evening to the next. It is better still if the flower opens one morning and persists until the evening of the following day, for one then has two days to enjoy it. Some recent breeding programmes have been designed to achieve this end.

Flowering Season

While the main flowering season for day lilies is during July and August, it is possible, by careful selection of species and varieties, to have day lilies in flower from late spring until the first frosts of autumn. The flowering seasons are denoted as follows:

    EE = extra early
    E   = early
    EM = early mid-season
    M   = mid-season
    LM = late mid-season
    L   = late
    VL = very late.

One of the **extra early** types is that very old favourite 'Maikoenigin' ('Queen of May'), which can probably be counted on as the start of the *Hemerocallis* season.

The **early** types are those that bloom three to five weeks before the main or mid-season, that is to say, they flower in early to mid-June. **Early mid-season** is from the end of June to mid-July, i.e. three weeks or so before the main season. **Mid-season** types bloom from mid-July to the beginning of August. The main season should not die away too quickly, but lead gradually into the **late mid-season**, when plants that bloom about three weeks later, i.e. around mid-August, take over. Any *Hemerocallis* still flowering at the end of August may be regarded as **late**. **Very late** varieties flower in September, giving a few last blooms into October.

Great progress has been made in extending the flowering season, and breeders have now developed hybrids that are not restricted merely to one period. Hence one increasingly finds descriptions such as 'E/EM' or 'EM/LM'. Such plants continue to produce new scapes and/or buds even after they have started to flower. 'Stella d'Oro' is an example of this kind, as is that quite splendid German hybrid 'Berliner Premiere' which, though listed as EE, blooms from early (E) to late mid-season (LM), that is to say, for at least ten weeks. On the other hand there are also reblooming day lilies (Re=reblooming) which means that having bloomed once, the plant rests for a short while and then begins a second blooming season. Reblooming is largely governed by a combination of heat and rainfall; if the summer is hot and there is sufficient rainfall, day lilies are likely to produce a new set of buds.

Growth Habits and Leaf Forms

Small flowers do not suit long scapes, nor large ones short scapes. But there is another important point, namely the way the scape branches, because large blooms do not look good if they are too close together and small ones are lost if they are too far apart. Branching is therefore also important, because a branched scape is capable of carrying more flowers than an unbranched one. A hybrid should have not less than ten buds and a multifloral type could well have up to 100.

Branching Habits

Branching is also desirable because flowers can appear simultaneously at different heights and thus give the plant a fuller appearance. The various modes or manners of branching are:

> top-branched
> well-branched
> low-branched
> multiple-branched.

The term **top-branched** denotes plants in which the branching occurs at the top of the scape. In the wild this phenomenon is typical of the species of the *middendorffii* group; in hybrids this is possibly not a desirable trait. It looks best if the branching starts level with the top of the foliage, and this is what we mean by the term **well branched**.

If, however, the scape does not overtop the foliage to any great extent, as happens with the miniature types, the scape starts to branch near the base within the foliage mass; this is called **low-branched**. If the branches themselves branch and rebranch two or three times giving a large number of stems, we have a **multiple-branched** plant. In each of the above instances the branch may lie close to the scape, more or less erect, or else grow out more laterally.

Length of Scape

Modern breeders look not only for ample branching, but also for an appropriate stem length, neither too long nor too short. The following measurements reflect recent tastes; ten years earlier they would have been 10cm taller:

> dwarf (less than 30cm)
> small (30–50cm)
> medium (51–80cm)
> tall (above 80cm).

One should not assume, however, that small flowers automatically entail small growth. 'Ed Murray', for instance, with a flower 10cm across, has a scape of 75cm; thus the flower is classed as small, whereas the scape is medium length. If you are looking for something to furnish a small garden, then attention should be paid not to the size of bloom, but rather to the length of the scape. Since nowadays more and more dwarf varieties are available, it should not prove difficult to find something suitable, even if space is at a premium.

Over-wintering

Another consideration is whether a particular plant is hardy or not. Day lilies fall into three groups:

> dormant
> evergreen
> semi-evergreen.

As a general rule evergreen types do not take particularly well to cold winter conditions, whereas dormant plants, which need a rest during winter, do. The term 'semi-evergreen' is really only meaningful in America, but since the term appears so often in catalogues and registrations it needs some explanation.

Those *Hemerocallis* plants whose

leaves turn brown and eventually die back in winter are said to be **dormant**. The plant then comes to life again in the spring. A plant is said to be 'hard dormant' if it dies back before the first frost, rather than because of it. Even in mild winters such plants remain below ground all winter.

This is not so with **semi-evergreens**, because their winter behaviour is entirely dependent on prevailing weather conditions. Frequently, therefore, only the upper part of the foliage will be killed by frosts and new foliage will keep appearing throughout the winter. In cold gardens semi-evergreens tend to behave much like dormant types.

Evergreen day lilies remain green even during the winter, but they are really bred for warmer climates such as those of California and Florida, for example. In the United Kingdom the constant alternation from frost to thaw and back causes the leaves to go mushy and this may weaken the plant, eventually even killing it.

Whether evergreen varieties will thrive in your garden is something that can be established only by trial and error. The other problem is that in cold, rainy summers day lilies bred for the southern states of America perform very poorly. If one is still determined to plant such varieties, because they will often give one glorious burst of blooms, the best time is in the spring. Then one at least has the safeguard that the plant will have taken root by the time winter sets in and may well have become acclimatised, because *Hemerocallis* does have this ability.

Day lily foliage can also vary in colour. Mostly the leaves are a healthy green, but the tone can vary from a light grass-green to a dark blue-green. If there is a yellowish tinge it means that the plant is either not all that healthy, or else that there might be some genetic problem. Whatever the cause, that plant should on no account be used for breeding. If there is any doubt about the health of a plant, the best thing is to compare it with a similar one in someone else's garden. A little fertiliser will also sometimes help to improve the condition of the foliage.

Diploid and Tetraploid Types

Hemerocallis species usually have a **diploid** chromosome complement, i.e. $2n=22$. However, there are four clones and varieties of the *fulva* group that possess an additional set of chromosomes; in other words they are **triploid**. Such a rise in the number of chromosomes can occur naturally, but usually natural causes tend to double the number of chromosomes and the plant then becomes **tetraploid**. (Thus we have $2n=$diploid, $3n=$triploid and $4n=$tetraploid, where 'n' denotes the number of chromosomes in a set.) Tetraploidy can result from sudden heat or cold, or from the fusion of unreduced sex cells. As there are no other polyploid species with more than two sets of chromosomes, apart from those mentioned above, all other tetraploid day lilies have arisen as a result of genetic engineering.

The chemical that is used for this purpose is colchicine, an exceedingly poisonous and dangerous extract from the autumn crocus (*Colchicum autumnale*). In 1937 it was discovered that this alkaloid can react with the protein tubulin, preventing the movement of the chromatids to the two poles during the metaphase of cell division. Instead of dividing they remain together in the cell nucleus, which results in the cell having twice the number of chromosomes. Even in the early stages of this discovery, day lily breeders began to experiment. Foremost among these were R. Schreiner, W.Q. Buck and H.P. Traub. The first success went to Schreiner in 1947 after treating a hybrid called 'Cressida' with colchicine, leading later to 'Brilliant Glow'. In 1949 Buck announced two tetraploid forms of the hybrids 'Soudan' and 'Kanapaha'. In each of these tetraploidy resulted from the treatment of a diploid with colchicine.

At the same time experiments were under way to try to intervene in cell division during the actual germination process of the seeds. The first truly tetraploid day lily developed in this way and with no diploid counterpart bloomed in 1949 and was called 'Tetra Starzynski'. The significance of these experiments was thought to be so momentous that it was decided in 1951 to accord the hybrid the status of a new species and it was registered as *H. washingtoniana*. It stood 1m high and was bronze-coloured with a pink sheen and an apricot eye; also it was evergreen. Tetraploidy can lead not only to bigger and more beautiful flowers, but also to improved winter-hardiness.

I do not propose to give a step-by-step explanation of the colchicine method, since a vast number of tetraploids have in the meantime become available and these may generally be crossed with each other. What has so far eluded the breeders is the development of triploid plants. There would be little sense in the production of such plants since they would be sterile. There are occasions, however, when one might want to develop a tetraploid form of a particularly successful diploid plant. To do this one treats the crown of the plant with colchicine and so obtains identical but bigger and stronger flowers. This method has produced 'tetra versions' of 'Empress Seal' and 'Green Flutter', for example, but they cost about five times as much as the diploid form. This kind of late inducement to tetraploidy can also produce chimaeras, which are plants with both tetraploid and diploid scapes on the same root system.

The advantages of tetraploid hybrids in practice are that not only are the flowers bigger and more substantial, but the plants are hardier. The flower colours are also more intense and with the greater number of chromosomes there is the possibility of even greater variety of colour combinations. (Incidentally, faster progress towards white and blue varieties has been made through the use of diploid forms.) The great advantage of tetraploidy is that it produces sturdier plants, more immune to diseases and pests and also more weather resistant. A disadvantage is the thickening of the scape, although this is occasionally necessary in order to carry the greater number of flowers. Another disadvantage is that tetraploids do not set seeds as easily as diploids.

MAKING THE CHOICE

Factors to Consider

There are now so many day lilies to choose from that knowing which ones to grow can be a problem. Nor can one ever be entirely sure that having made the choice it will be the right one. A picture in a catalogue may look attractive, but it does not really tell much about the quality of a plant. The previous chapter may have helped to narrow the choice, but the following points are of special importance:

- Do the flowers remain open all day or longer, or do they start to fade in the late afternoon?
- Is the particular variety right for the particular garden? What size is the plant: small, medium or giant?
- Are the flowers to your taste? Not every plant in the various lists is necessarily what you might consider beautiful.
- Are the flowers weather-proof: do they tend to fade in strong sunlight or does the pigment scatter in rain?
- Is the plant of the extended blooming or the reblooming sort?
- Is the flower fragrant?

Catalogues can give only a very poor guide as to which day lilies to grow. They are useful guides to size of the flower or the plant and the flowering season, but they are usually produced by nurserymen to sell their wares. Their praises may be fulsome and they seldom mention any failings. Besides, colour reproduction is often misleading for purely technical reasons. The best way of choosing day lilies is to see them growing in gardens. In Britain there are on-going trials of day lilies at the Royal Horticultural Society's garden at Wisley, near Woking in Surrey. They may be seen growing throughout the garden there, as well as at the Royal Botanic Gardens, Kew, at the botanic gardens of most universities, at the garden of the Northern Horticultural Society, and in the private gardens of several members of the British Hosta and Hemerocallis Society (BHHS) (see appendix).

It is always best to see the plants in gardens or nurseries and to seek the advice of the people actually engaged in growing them.

If it is not possible to see specimens of the plants in which you are interested, then you might find the following tips of help. The chapter entitled 'Propagation and Selection of Hybrids' is worth studying carefully, because all the best British and European varieties are listed and they compare well with imported varieties. Members of the American Hemerocallis Society (AHS), the German 'Gesellschaft der Staudenfreunde' (Gds) and the British Hosta and Hemerocallis Society (BHHS) have access to an annual list of the most popular varieties.

With day lilies, as with other things, value and price are not necessarily the same thing. In their first season new varieties from America usually fetch around 50–100 US dollars, but after they have been on the market for three or four years the price drops by about half. One can never tell in advance how a new variety will be received, and the dearer it is the more critical is the buyer.

The main thing with a day lily is that it should be beautiful, and this is a matter of taste. Furthermore it should possess some special qualities that other similar sorts do not possess. It ought, for example, to flower profusely and over a long period, the scape should be well-branched and its height commensurate with the size and shape of the flowers. These in turn should be substantial or graceful and elegant, weather-proof, and they should open properly even after a cold night; the flower should not fade in sunlight, nor the pigment scatter after heavy rain. If the plant is of the kind that cleans itself, that is yet another bonus. 'Cleaning itself' means that the flowers fall from the plant once they are over. Finally the plant must be healthy and vigorous, maintaining from year to year its ability to bloom.

These are not just theoretical targets, for most of the new hybrids possess these characteristics. This is why, in the descriptions that follow, the older types of plants are mentioned only if they have endured the test of time. Complete novelties that may catch the fancy of the moment are mostly omitted, for all too often they display shortcomings after two or three years in the garden. Most of the plants described are therefore those that have proved themselves and that are commercially available.

Yellow is not just Yellow

Most *Hemerocallis* hybrids are yellow, as is borne out by the majority of AHS prize-winners. Plants with flowers of this colour are generally not complicated: their flowers open easily, they usually bloom over a long period and they are often scented. Even so there is among them a great diversity of heights and flower sizes, as well as flower shapes. As the title of this section points out, the general term 'yellow' encompasses many individual shades of that colour: pale yellow, light yellow, sulphur-yellow, lemon-yellow, mid-yellow, cadmium-yellow and orange-yellow. Orange, brownish, light brown, copper, amber and date-coloured ought also to be included in this range.

Among the historic hybrids is a great number of Stout Medal winners that are now no longer available in the trade. There are, however, other old-fashioned hybrids that have lost none of their popularity; although long superseded in shape and style and colour, they are still stocked by many nurseries and feature in lists of British and European favourites. 'Ava Michelle' and 'Hyperion' are two such. Furthermore, there are a number of older prize-winners like 'Cartwheels' and 'Full Reward' that can hold their own against modern hybrids. They therefore deserve their listing under 'Large-flowered varieties'. Among the small and miniature types there are three older varieties that to my mind, are a must for any garden: 'Corky', Golden Chimes' and 'McPick'.

Historic Varieties

Apricot	(1893 Yeld)	orange-apricot, tall, large
Aten	(1952 Kraus)	orange flowers with narrow tepals
August Orange	(1946 Stout)	small-flowered, late *multiflora* type with orange, bell-shaped flowers
Ava Michelle	(1960 Flory)	tight, circular golden-yellow blooms of good substance, green throat
Banbury Cinnamon	(1965 Brummit)	cinnamon-coloured narrow tepals, dilated yellow throat
Dauntless	(1935 Stout)	small orange-yellow blooms on tall scapes
Dorothy McDade	(1941 Sass)	bright orange-yellow blooms
Double Honey	(1963 Kraus)	small, double golden-yellow blooms with strong green throat
Fairy Wings	(1953 Lester)	light yellow very large blooms on exceptionally tall scapes
Green Valley	(1955 Fischer)	tall plant with bright greenish-yellow blooms, strongly fragrant
Hesperus	(1940 Sass)	light orange-yellow blooms, taller than Hesperus
High Noon	(1948 Milliken)	tall, re-blooming variety with deep orange-yellow flowers
Hortensia	(1964 Branch)	golden-yellow round bloom, compact, with wavy edge
Hyperion	(1924 Mead)	masses of light yellow blooms in mid to late summer, very fragrant
Kindly Light	(1950 Bechtold)	*the* classic yellow spider shape
Lona Eaton Miller	(1960 Kraus)	mid-yellow miniature blooms, pale violet median stripe

Marion Vaughn	(1951 Smith)	many light yellow blooms in mid to late summer, very fragrant
Naranja	(1948 Wheeler)	giant mid-yellow flowers with orange centres
Playboy	(1954 Wheeler)	strong orange 'Naranja' seedling with rounder flowers
Reverend Traub	(1959 Traub)	cadmium-yellow, one of the first tetraploids
Revolute	(1944 Sass)	yellow blooms with broad, strongly reflexed tepals
Shooting Star	(1951 Hall)	greenish-yellow star-shaped blooms on well-branched scapes
Suzie Wong	(1962 Kennedy)	small flowers, bright yellow, green throat
Thelma Perry	(1925 Perry)	well-branched scapes bearing blooms of clear canary-yellow, very fragrant
Thumbelina	(1954 Fischer)	dwarf variety with orange bells
Tinker Bell	(1955 Stevens)	early variety with orange-yellow miniature flowers
Willard Gardner	(1969 Lambert)	large greenish-yellow blooms, very fragrant
Whichford	(not registered)	clear lemon-yellow, exquisite fragrance

Large-flowered Varieties

Apple Crisp	(1982 Guidry)	rich burnt copper, green throat
Bernard Thompson	(1967 Coe)	late mid-season, orange, tall scapes, evergreen
Betty Woods	(1980 Kirchhoff)	chinese-yellow paeony-type double with distinct green throat
Bright Spangles	(1956 Baker)	unusual combination of bright orange-red, flecked yellow
Brocaded Gown	(1979 Millikan)	very ruffled, round, palest lemon-cream
Burning Daylight	(1957 Fischer)	deep orange blooms on tall scapes
By Myself	(1971 Peck)	round, broadly wavy golden margin, tetraploid
Cabbage Flower	(1985 Kirchhoff)	clear lemon-yellow, very double, ruffled form
Cajun Gambler	(1986 Guidry)	burnt-orange and bronze-yellow blend, ruffled, evergreen

Cartwheels	(1956 Fay)	round, flat, clear golden-yellow
Chestnut Lane	(1979 Blyth)	light golden-brown, darker chestnut-brown eye-zone, fluted and ruffled, lightly fragrant
Chicago Sunrise	(1969 Marsh/Klehm)	long-blooming mid-yellow
Chinese Autumn	(1973 Munson)	coral-orange blend, pale orange throat
Colour Me Mellow	(1988 Blyth)	lemon-apricot and melon bi-tone, orchid midrib
Condilla	(1979 Gooms)	golden-yellow double, well-filled medium-sized flowers (layer-on-layer)
Darrell	(1981 Durio)	light butter-yellow, chartreuse throat, evergreen
Dorethe Louise	(1976 Peck)	greenish-yellow blooms, darker green throat, tetraploid
Eidelweiss	(1974 Viette)	pale yellow, heavy bloomer
Ellen Christine	(1987 Crochet)	blend of cream-yellow and pink, green-gold throat, very ruffled double
Frozen Jade	(1975 Sellers)	lemon-yellow, extended blooming, strong fragrance, tetraploid
Full Reward	(1975 McVicker)	cadmium-yellow, round blooms, very broad tepals
Galena Moon	(1981 Bryant)	lemon-yellow flowers, yellow throat, extended blooming, fragrant
Golden Prize	(1968 Peck)	strong golden-yellow blooms, crêped, tetraploid
Golden Scroll	(1983 Guidry)	rich golden-orange, exceptional ruffling, reblooming
Green Glitter	(1964 Harrison)	greenish-yellow, ruffled blooms, chartreuse throat
Green Puff	(1977 Spalding)	very green, tinged yellow, dark green throat
Hudson Valley	(1971 Peck)	greenish-yellow blooms, fragrance award-winner
Ida Duke Miles	(1986 Webster)	lemon-yellow, heavy substance, fragrance award-winner
Jerome	(1979 Spalding)	light-orange, darker eye-zone, green throat, extended blooming
Lemon Mint	(1970 Rudolf)	pale yellow, highly fragrant
Limited Edition	(1969 Lambert)	giant chrome-yellow, extra-early blooming

MAKING THE CHOICE

Mauna Loa	(1976 Roberts)	tangerine-copper-gold blend, narrow red margin, tetraploid
Mary Todd	(1967 Fay)	golden-yellow self, very large flowers
Nova	(1962 Lester)	pale yellow, fragrant
Northbrook Star	(1968 Fay)	very large, star-shaped mid-yellow flowers, tall, tetraploid
Norton Orange	(1971 Coe)	strong orange-yellow starry flowers, tetraploid, evergreen
Pat Mercer	(1982 Joyner)	orange, lighter halo, green throat, noctural, semi-evergreen
Showamber	(1988 Blyth)	rich orange, tangerine throat, evergreen, tetraploid
Silkwood	(1985 Chesnik)	light brown self, deeper eye-zone, tetraploid
Siloam Mama	(1982 Henry)	large yellow flowers with short pedicels, very fragrant
Windsong	(1974 Bryant)	cream-pink blend, cream throat, fragrant
Winning Ways	(1963 Wild)	light yellow, green throat, triangular

Small-flowered Varieties

Butterscotch Ruffles	(1978 Harling)	buff-yellow, peach overtones, very floriferous
Camden Gold Dollar	(1983 Yancey)	deep golden-yellow, round and ruffled
David Paul French	(1979 Powell)	golden-yellow
Double Cutie	(1972 Brown)	chartreuse-yellow double, reblooming
Eenie Allegro	(1981 Aden)	rose edges over cream-apricot, looks yellow, rebloomer in hot climates
Eeenie Weenie	(1976 Aden)	mid-yellow recurved blooms
Everblooming Doll	(1978 Lenington)	bright-yellow flowers on low scapes, semi-evergreen
Green Flutter	(1964 Williamson)	circular, canary-yellow blooms, green throats, semi-evergreen
Happy Returns	(1986 Apps)	canary yellow, consistent rebloomer
Hi de Ho	(1978 Kennedy)	honey, gold and orange blend, brownish towards centre
Kevin	(1976 McEwen)	bitone, cinnamon-coloured, golden throat, rare colour

MAKING THE CHOICE

Jenny Wren	(1959 Fischer)	near-brown flowers, yellow throat
Lemon Bells	(1969 Coe)	clear yellow, trumpet-shaped flowers, very floriferous, evergreen
Little Deeke	(1980 Guidry)	orange-gold, green throat, crêped petals, fragrant
Little Greenie	(1972 Winniford)	strong green-yellow, green throat
McPick	(1957 Lenington)	circular, pure gold-yellow flowers, dark mahogany buds
Wynn	(1975 Criswell)	yellow self, green throat, extended blooming

Miniature-flowered Varieties

Bertie Ferris	(1969 Winniford)	date-orange-coloured flowers, lighter edges and midrib
Bitsy	(1963 Warner)	tiny yellow flowers throughout the summer
Butterpat	(1970 Kennedy)	yellow, fragrant flowers that open in the evening
Corky	(1959 Fischer)	lemon-yellow bells on profusely-branched mahogany scapes
Curls	(1958 Kraus)	yellow flowers, tinged apricot, wavy edges
Daily Bread	(1973 Hager)	egg-yolk yellow flowers, elegant low scapes, extended blooming
Golden Chimes	(1954 Fischer)	gold-yellow trumpet shaped flowers on well-branched scapes, extended blooming
Irish Elf	(1978 Hudson)	lemon-chartreuse, rapid increaser, evergreen
Mini Stella	(1983 Jablonski)	bright-yellow self, smaller and lighter-coloured flowers than Stella d'Oro
Pojo	(1972 Winniford)	early, reblooming, golden-yellow double
Puddin	(1972 Kennedy)	mid-yellow flowers, green throats on short scapes
Raindrop	(1972 Kennedy)	light-yellow self, fragrant, semi-evergreen
Song Sparrow	(1979 Griesbach/Klehm)	orange-yellow camellia-type blooms, edged ivory
Stella d'Oro	(1975 Jablonski)	continuous blooming variety with golden-yellow circular flowers
Tiny Pumpkin	(1975 Hudson)	orange blooms, green throats

Red Varieties for Colder Climates (British and European)

There are as many shades of red as there are of yellow. They range from the dull brownish rusty-reds bred from *H. fulva*, and then run through the whole range from orange and flame, light red, carmine, wine, dark red and dark mahogany, to a colour that is almost black. Purple varieties with a high blue content are listed on p. 87–91. Fewer red varieties than yellow varieties have so far won awards. However, those plants listed under the heading 'Historic Varieties' are good garden plants, but it is particularly in this colour range that the differences between them and modern hybrids are most marked.

With none of the other colours, except purple and violet, does one have to be quite so careful about weather hardiness as with red day lily varieties. Red day lily flowers are inclined to become spotty after cold nights and they do not generally tolerate rainy conditions well. Evergreen reds tend, on the whole, to do less well than the dormant types, since the evergreen varieties are mostly bred for a warmer climate, but 'Amadeus' and 'Apple Tart', both semi-evergreens, do exceptionally well in gardens in southern England.

Historic Varieties

Name	Year/Breeder	Description
Alan	(Claar 1953)	cherry-red, greenish-yellow throat
Banbury Signal	(1964 Brummit)	signal-red, starry flower, orange-yellow throat
Bess Ross	(1951 Claar)	brilliant red, extremely weatherproof
Bourbon Kings	(1968 Wild)	substantial dark-red flower, green-yellow throat
Buzz Bomb	(1961 Hall)	low-growing, bright velvety-red
Cherry Ripe	(1959 Brummit)	starry, light-red flowers
Christmas Carol	(1971 Wild)	velvety carmine flower, green throat
Crimson Pirate	(1951 Sass)	free-flowering, small red, starry blooms
Haymaker	(1961 Hall)	strong red, not over-large flower with green-yellow throat
Jet Scarlet	(1967 Coe)	brilliant scarlet-red
Kathleen Ormerod	(never registered)	bright red
Little Trump	(1964 Hall)	bright red velvety flower with wavy edges
Little Tyke	(1962 Wild)	well-branched scape, bright red sort with green-yellow throat

Oriental Ruby	(1968 Fischer)	weather-proof sort, bright carmine flower, green throat
Potentate	(1943 Nesmith)	almost black, medium-large flowers on tall scape
Red Cup	(1954 Douglas)	small mid-red flowers on tall scapes, semi-evergreen
Red Mittens	(1966 Heinemann)	mid-red miniature type, many awards
Red Precious	(1968 Coe)	medium-sized brilliant red, star-like in form
Regal Air	(1963 Wild)	matt blood-red colour, plastic-like texture
Ruby Wine	(1971 Coe)	velvety, dark wine-red self
Sail On	(1964 Claar/Parry*)	bright red, long-blooming sort with medium-sized flowers
Sammy Russell	(1951 Russell)	small tile-red starry flowers, divide old plants
Skiatook Cardinal	(1960 Hancock)	velvety rich red flower with darker centre
Stafford	(1959 Randall)	brilliant red, prominent white midrib, star-like form
Tang	(1964 Lambert)	small ox-blood flowers, semi-evergreen but very hardy

Large-flowered Varieties

American Revolution	(1972 Wild)	velvety, black-red starry flowers on lowish scapes, very floriferous
Amadeus	(1981 Kirchhoff)	scarlet self, yellow-green throat, semi-evergreen, tetraploid
Apple Tart	(1974 Hughes)	rich scarlet, weather-resistant flowers, tetraploid
Bald Eagle	(1979)	deep red, yellow throat
Bruno Muller	(1974 Coe)	bright orange-red, tall scapes, tetraploid
Cherry Cheeks	(1968 Peck)	cherry-red, white midrib, near-black anthers
Chicago Apache	(1981 Marsh/Klehm)	round, ruffled, bright scarlet self
Chicago Ruby	(1977 Marsh)	carmine self, green throat, semi-evergreen
Dawn Piper	(1987 Elliott)	rose-red self, deep-red eye-zone, yellow-green throat, evergreen
Dewey Roquemore	(1972 Warner)	round, recurved, dark-red flowers, faint black halo, green throat, tetraploid

*Claar was the hybridiser and Parry undertook the rearing and selection

MAKING THE CHOICE

Douglas Dale	(1968 Peck)	strong, weather-resistant red, tetraploid
Fanny Stadler	(1970 Helms)	rich red, green throat
Galena Holiday	(1980 Blocher)	good weather-resistant red, tetraploid
Hemlock	(1979 Griesbach/Klehm)	wide-petalled, sunfast, rich clear red, brilliant-green throat
James Marsh	(1978 Marsh/Klehm)	scarlet, yellow-green throat, very ruffled form, tetraploid
Jim Cooper	(1968 Lambert)	very large carmine flowers, green throats
King Haiglar	(1972 Kennedy)	wide, trumpet-shaped velvety scarlet, yellow-green throat
Lusty Lealand	(1970 Peck)	good mid-red, striking orange backs to petals and sepals, evergreen but definitely weatherproof, tetraploid
Mallard	(1979 Griesbach/Klehm)	ruby-red
Margaret Marlatt	(1968 Lambert)	deep-red flowers, ruffled edges, darker halo
Norton Hall	(1967 Coe)	velvety-red, broad tepals, green-yellow throat, tetraploid, hot weatherproof.
Red Roque	(1977 McKinney)	weatherproof, strong-red flowers with velvet sheen, semi-evergreen, chartreuse throat, fragrant
Scarlock	(1974 Peck)	red self, yellow-green throat, tetraploid
Siloam Red Velvet	(1975 Henry)	velvety-red self
Wally Nance	(1976 Wild)	velvety, bright ruby-red, fine white edging around a yellow throat

Small-flowered Varieties

Christmas Is	(1979 Yancey)	scarlet, wide, brilliant chartreuse throat, reblooming
Cranberry Baby	(1986 Croker)	cranberry-red, deeper eye, deeper midribs
Crimson Icon	(1982 Hudson)	rich rose-red, ruffled, rapid increaser
Double Razzle Dazzle	(1974 Brown)	red double self, green throat, evergreen
Double Flash-Splash	(1983 Brown)	bright tomato red, ruffled and layered double
Ed Murray	(1971 Grovatt)	one of the 'blackest' reds, green throat, very tall scapes

Eenie Fanfare	(1981 Aden)	velvety-red blooms, white edge, very floriferous
Little Business	(1971 Maxwell)	red self, green throat, low-growing
Little Fat Dazzler	(1979 Lankart)	unusual light-red, yellow throat
Lord Camden	(1974 Kennedy)	cherry-red, green throat
Pardon Me	(1982 Apps)	deep-red self, yellow-green throat, prolific bloomer
Siloam Ribbon Candy	(1982 Henry)	rose-red, deeper eye-zone, ruffled edge
Siloam Show Girl	(1981 Henry)	mid-red, with deeper red eye, green throat

Miniature-flowered Varieties

Jekyll Jewell	(1976 Yancey)	light-red flowers, green throats, semi-evergreen
Little Red Hen	(1979 Apps)	small red flowers on tall scapes
Little Zinger	(1979 Lambert)	red, conspicuous green throat, low-growing
Siloam Pocket Size	(1983 Henry)	rose-red, red halo
Siloam Red Toy	(1975 Henry)	cherry-red self, bell-shaped flowers on short pedicels

Pink and Related Tones

Pink is one of the most imprecise of colour descriptions and pink day lilies have a strong undertone of yellow, though a few also contain a large amount of blue in their pink. To try to make the descriptions more meaningful, the following terms have been used: pale pink, flesh-pink, pink-melon, salmon-pink, rose, raspberry-pink, lavender, orchid-pink, rich pink and rose-pink.

Many of the pink hybrids become more attractive by being marked, that is eyed, haloed or edged. Some of these are described later. Very light-pink varieties, such as 'Cindy Marie', often have darker veins on their flower segments, or midribs, which add interest. Some have raised white midribs. There are also many ruffled pink varieties, such as 'Dance Ballerina Dance', which remains expensive even though it has been around since the mid 1970s. Before deciding to buy such expensive plants, one needs to consider whether the variety is to be used for breeding purposes because, in the colder weather conditions of northern Britain and parts of Europe, the blooms tend not to fully open. Their value lies rather in the fact that they make a good parent plant for hybridizing ruffled types. Some of the light pink shades such as 'Fairy Tale Pink' and 'Janet Gayle' need a great deal of strong sunlight to produce the pink shade the breeders intended.

Apart from the range of pinks mentioned above, included with pink are also all the very palest shades and nearly whites. Besides the light colour tones for which there are no individual descriptions, there are also the pastel colours such as melon, peach and apricot. The first time any of these colours was seen in Europe was at the International Horticultural Exhibition in Hamburg in 1963. An apricot-coloured hybrid called 'George Cunningham' attracted much attention at the time and was awarded the Silver Medal: it is still popular today. Much to the credit of Countess von Zeppelin's nursery and Norton Hall Nursery in Britain, these 'new' colours were catalogued and included in their lists. Nowadays, hybrids in these pale shades enjoy a great deal of popularity and blend in very well with other garden plants.

Even European breeders benefit here, for, as can be seen from the evaluation table for new hybrids on p. 109, pink and related tones are more highly rated than yellow types. The latter are common enough, after all.

Circular shapes and ruffled edges come into their own among the pinks.

Historic Varieties

Apricot Angel	(1963 Holman)	small-flowered, pinkish-melon-coloured with semi-evergreen foliage
Bambi Doll	(1965 Wild)	small light pink flowers with green throats
Cadence	(1960 Fay/Hardy)	very pale melon
Edna Spalding	(1962 Spalding)	starry flowers of a very pretty pink
Elaine Strutt	(1969 Coe)	medium-sized ruffled blooms of a clear pink, tetraploid
Frances Fay	(1957 Fay)	medium-sized, melon-coloured, free-flowering sort
George Cunningham	(1957 Hall)	blended melon-coloured, still worth growing
Love that Pink	(1962 Hall)	medium-sized, pure pink sort
Lula Mae Purnell	(1961 Kraus/Shilling)	small peach-coloured blooms with green throats
May Hall	(1960 Hall)	rich rosy-peach flowers with bluish-pink flush
Melon Balls	(1960 Wild)	strong melon with orchid-pink tinge
Michelle Coe	(1969 Coe)	creamy-melon, midribs touched lavender, blooms wide and frilled

Multnomah	(1954 Kraus)	apricot blooms with light pink tinge
Nob Hill	(1962 Hall)	bicolour pale pink blooms with lavender flush
Penelope Vestey	(1969 Coe)	large pink with deeper halo, lemon throat, very floriferous
Pink Lightning	(1962 Hall)	blended pink variety
Prima Donna	(1946 Taylor)	pink sort with different tones on sepals and petals
Ruffled Pinafore	(1948 Milliken)	bitone, light orange-pink flowers
Salmon Sheen	(1950 Taylor)	evergreen, salmon-pink sort
Step Forward	(1963 Hall)	blended pink flowers with small yellow throats
Summer Splendour	(1965 Reckamp)	large apricot flower with orchid-pink median stripe
Toyland	(1965 Reckamp)	tiny apricot-coloured bells with strong throats
Winsome Lady	(1964 Gates)	melon and pink blend with chartreuse throat

Large-flowered Varieties

Becky Lynn	(1977 Guidry)	blended rose flowers with green throat, fragrant
Blue Happiness	(1975 Spalding)	rose flower with blue edge and green throat
Cenla Triumph	(1979 Tanner)	pink with gold edge and lavender median stripe, tetraploid
Chicago Cameo	(1976 Marsh)	semi-evergreen, shell-pink sort with green throat tetraploid
Cindy Marie	(1977 Durio)	light pink, ruffled flower with green throat
Clarence Simon	(1966 MacMillan)	pink-melon flower with green throat, evergreen
Coming Your Way	(1968 Wild)	medium-sized fuchsia-pink flower, mandarin-coloured heart
Dancing Shiva	(1974 Moldovan)	mid-pink blend with yellow-green throat, tetraploid
Egyptian Spice	(1969 Reckamp)	copper and orange blend with green throat, tetraploid
Elizabeth Yancey	(1973 Yancey/Harrison)	early, reblooming, slightly ruffled, pale pink variety
Etched in Gold	(1971 Peck)	pink-melon variety with gold edge, tetraploid
Fairy Tale Pink	(1980 Pierce)	cream-pink blend, green throat, very ruffled

Florissant Miss	(1982 Harris)	pastel-pink ruffled bloom with pale green throat
Frank Gladney	(1982 Durio)	hot coral pink
Heather Green	(1968 Peck)	pink-melon blend, bright-green throat, tetraploid
Janet Gayle	(1976 Guidry)	early, cream-pink blend, frilled, reblooming
Martha Adams	(1979 Spalding)	light rose-pink, green throat, frilled edges
Ming Porcelain	(1981 Kirchhoff)	wide pastel ivory-peach blend
My Belle	(1973 Durio)	flesh-coloured, ruffled edges, green throat, evergreen
Nile Crane	(1980 Munson)	pastel bluish lavender, wide cream-green throat
Pa Pa Gulino	(1977 Durio)	double, silvery-flesh-pink, ruffled, tetraploid
Panfield Charm	(P. Coe – not registered)	clear mid-pink, tetraploid
Pink Circle	(1981 Spalding)	bright pink, deeper pink eye-zone, round, ruffled
Pink Corduroy	(1984 Stamile)	light pink, white midribs, green throat
Rose Emily	(1982 Pierce)	rose self, green throat, recurved petals, semi-evergreen
Ruffled Apricot	(1972 Baker)	apricot with lavender-pink midrib, heavy substance, ruffled, tetraploid
Sari	(1973 Munson)	orchid-pink, cream throat, semi-evergreen (tetraploid form now available)
Silver Ice	(1984 Munson)	pale ice-pink blushed palest lavender, evergreen, tetraploid
Silver Veil	(1977 Munson)	pale bluish silvery-lavender self, wide lemon throat, evergreen, tetraploid
Smoky Mountain Autumn	(1986 Guidry)	blend of lavender-rose, with copper-bronze overtones, evergreen
Tonia Gay	(1984 Spalding/Guillory)	baby ribbon pink over white, greenish-yellow throat
Yesterday's Memories	(1976 Spalding)	blue-toned mid-pink, green throat, slightly ruffled, evergreen

Small-flowered Varieties

Blushing Maiden	(1982 Kirchhoff)	bicolour, hot pink petals, recurved, ivory sepals, evergreen

Chorus Line	(1983 Kirchhoff)	clear medium pink, wide rose eye-band, green throat, fragrant
Frosted Pink Ice	(1987 Stamile)	blush-pink self, white midribs, yellow-green throat
Ice Castles	(1985 Salter)	ivory-peach blend, long-blooming period, evergreen
Lady Inara	(1956 Hall)	pink, melon and cream blend, very free-blooming
Lullaby Baby	(1975 Spalding)	ice-pink, ruffled, round flowers, semi-evergreen
Luxury Lace	(1959 Spalding)	lavender-pink, bright-green throat
Pink Corsage	(1989 Guidry)	melon-pink double, green throat, fragrant
Tropical Toy	(1984 Hudson)	creamy-peach, frilled and ruffled, semi-evergreen

Miniature-flowered Varieties

Dainty Dreamer	(1983 Hudson)	blend of ivory, yellow and cream, pale pink highlights, semi-evergreen
Fairy Frosting	(1980 Hudson)	ivory and pale frosty-pink blend, evergreen
Garden Puppet	(1975 Hudson)	ivory and pink blend, citron-green throat
Little Celena	(1970 Williamson)	rose, green throat, evergreen
Little Pink Charmer	(1980 Cruse)	pink self, green throat, evergreen
Winnie The Pooh	(1964 Wild)	peach, yellow pastel blend

Near-white and Blue-toned Varieties

It may seem odd to treat blue and white together, both here and in the section 'Special Projects' in the next chapter. The reason, quite simply, is that there are no wild species or forms in either of these colours. White and blue hybrids are wholly and solely the product of the hybridiser's art. Just as there are those day lily growers who do not particularly care for the double varieties, so there are those who remain unmoved by blues or whites, perhaps because neither is available as an absolutely pure colour.

The so-called white sorts mostly have a tinge of some other colour in them. Hence all those varieties that could be termed 'light-coloured' are also included. The hues involved are ivory, yellowish, pink or bluish, the latter being rare, because blue acts as an intensifier of white (as in washing powders). Nevertheless, it can be claimed that the objective has been achieved: it is no longer difficult to find a white variety. In my experience, however, the vigour of the plants has suffered through constant crossing and recrossing, so that they do not, apart from 'Joan Senior' and 'Irongate Iceberg', reproduce as rapidly as do other colour groups, and they can be more prone to diseases.

Nor are the blues truly blue either. That which is extolled as 'blue' in American catalogues does not really justify such a description. Nor can one rely on coloured pictures, for all sorts of things are possible with photo-processing. At present blues are really lavender, lilac, mauve or purple. Often the beauty of such varieties is emphasised by blooms that are bicolour or have an eye-zone.

Blues and whites should not be rejected simply because pure colours have not yet been achieved. For progress to be made in plant breeding it is necessary to find ways of achieving these objectives. On the other hand it is questionable whether all the hybrids produced along the route are actually good garden plants.

Historic Varieties

White:

Guardian Angel	(1964 Core)	small-flowered, cream-white with green throat
Ice Carnival	(1967 Childs)	highly commendable because it is almost white, robust and very fragrant
Satin Glass	(1960 Fay/Hardy)	flowers have mother-of-pearl shimmer with green throat
Silver Fan	(1968 Peck)	very pale yellow flowers almost white, tetraploid
White Cloud	(1967 Traub/Hardy)	nearly-white, very large blooms, tetraploid
White Emeralds	(1974 Coe)	cream-coloured sort, also sold as 'Cream Emeralds'
White Formal	(1965 Lenington)	triangular, fairly white, medium-sized blooms
White Jade	(1954 Fay)	very light blooms with pink flush, grows well

Blue:

Catherine Woodbery	(1967 Childs)	large flowers of pretty lavender hue, tall scapes
Elsie Kearney	(1967 Lambert)	lavender-coloured flowers with large green throat
Lavender Flight	(1963 Spalding)	strong lavender colour, meagre growth, semi-evergreen

Large-flowered Varieties
White:

Agape Love	(1975 Spalding)	ivory-cream, pink midribs, green throat, semi-evergreen
Astolat	(1974 Peck)	very near-white, well-balanced circular shape, tetraploid
Blanco Real	(1978 Harris)	ivory-white, extended blooming, semi-evergreen
Call to Remembrance	(1969 Spalding)	near-white self, ice-pink highlights, green throat, semi-evergreen
Gentle Shepherd	(1980 Yancey)	to date, one of the 'whitest', near white self, yellow-green throat
Irongate Glacier	(1971 Sellers)	near-white self, semi-evergreen
Irongate Iceberg	(1972 Sellers)	near-white self, green throat, semi-evergreen
Joan Senior AM	(1977 Durio)	near-white, circular shape, delicate green throat, evergreen
Kazuq	(1986 Jinkerson)	creamy-near white, green throat, evergreen
Light The Way	(1976 Yancey)	icy-white, light-green throat, semi-evergreen
Luminous Jewel	(1974 Childs)	near-white, mint-green throat
Serene Madonna	(1972 Childs)	near-white, green-yellow throat, flat and round
White Temptation	(1978 Sellers)	near-white self, green throat

Blue:

Apple Court Damson	(1992 Grenfell)	velvety damson-purple, very floriferous, fragrant
Benchmark	(1982 Munson)	pale pastel lavender, cream throat, evergreen
Brent Gabriel	(1981 Guidry)	double purple bitone, white watermarking, evergreen
Chicago Knobby	(1974 Marsh)	purple bitone, darker throat, high blue content, tetraploid
Chicago Queen	(1974 Marsh)	lavender-blue, purple eye-zone, tetraploid
Chicago Royal Robe	(1974 Marsh/Klehm)	deep purple, green throat, lightly fragrant
Chicago Weathermaster	(1974 Marsh)	purple bitone, lighter-purple eye-zone, tetraploid
Double Grapette	(1976 Brown)	dark purple self, green throat, reblooming
Empress Seal	(1975 Moldovan)	lavender-blue flowers with chalky-white eye, induced tetraploid

Graceful Eye	(1981 Spalding)	bright clear lavender, purple halo, green throat
Mountain Violet	(1974 Munson)	rich violet-purple, darker throat, evergreen
Olive Bailey Langdon	(1974 Munson)	deep purple, bright-green throat, tetraploid
Prairie Blue Eyes	(1970 Marsh)	lavender, near-blue eye-zone, green throat
Royal Heritage	(1978 Munson)	plum-blue flowers, lighter throat, tetraploid
Russian Rhapsody	(1973 Munson)	deep purple-violet, yellow-green throat, semi-evergreen
Sebastian	(1978 Williams)	vivid purple, low-growing
Super Purple	(1979 Dove)	dark reddish-purple self, citron-green throat, semi-evergreen
Swirling Water	(1978 Carpenter)	velvety purple, creamy-white splash, green throat

Small-flowered Varieties

White:

Hope Diamond	(1968 McMillan)	near-white, yellowish tinge, low-growing
Little Melissa	(1980 Durio)	near-white, green throat
Little Snowy	(1982 Childs)	near-white, low-growing, long-blooming
Mary Crocker	(1982 Crocker)	ivory, jade-green throat
Mosel	(1982 Kirchhoff)	creamy, near-white, semi-evergreen
Netsuke	(1973 Moldovan)	light cream, green-yellow throat

Blue:

Barbary Corsair	(1980 Hudson)	rich violet-plum-purple self
Button Box	(1975 Irish)	clear lavender-blue, tetraploid
Dark Elf	(1979 Hudson)	rich plum-purple, semi-evergreen
Little Nicky	(1978 Durio)	lilac-pink, nile-green throat
Little Violet Lace	(1979 Spalding)	lilac-rose-lavender, lighter edging
Little Wart	(1964 Spalding)	strong lavender-blue, green throat
Meadow Sprite	(1979 Hudson)	lilac-rose lavender, deeper eye-band, green-yellow throat, fragrant, evergreen
Siloam Purple Plum	(1970 Henry)	wine-red, blue undertone, green throat

Miniature-flowered Varieties

Blue:

Fox Grape	(1973 Allwood)	grape-blue, lighter eye-band
Kokeshi	(1973 Moldovan)	blackberry shade
Little Grapette	(1970 Williamson)	dark grape-blue, yellow-green throat
Water Witch	(1979 Hudson)	lavender-purple

Patterns for Enhancement (eyed, banded, haloed or watermarked)

The list of award-winners in the next section indicates that patterned varieties are very much in demand at the moment, especially among the small and miniature-flowered varieties. Among these the hybrids of Pauline Henry are outstanding; they all have the prefix 'Siloam' after her nursery at Siloam Springs, Arkansas, USA. Not all, but a great many, are low-growing, small-flowered varieties with conspicuous and quite unusual colour patterns.

Usually the flowers are circular as well as ruffled and they really do make a very handsome addition to a sunny garden. They are becoming increasingly available in Britain and Europe though unfortunately still in rather too limited a quantity. Many are bred for sunny climates and so will not perform well in British gardens, so the trialling of as many of these varieties as possible at the RHS garden at Wisley, and the National Reference Collection of Small and Miniature Cultivars on the Isle of Wight is very important.

Several nurseries also have them growing in display borders, and members of the British Hosta and Hemerocallis Society are amassing good collections, and the Society will be happy to give advice on selecting these day lilies as and when it becomes available.

There are, of course, some older varieties that are just as worthwhile, but most of the patterned day lilies are of the smaller varieties. This is not so much because nothing came of attempts at breeding large-flowered patterned varieties, but rather because the early results were not pleasing. Now the picture is different and several breeders, especially R.W. Munson of Wimberley Way Gardens, Florida, USA, have raised many beautiful varieties.

Up until now breeders in Europe have not shown a great deal of interest in raising these patterned types. So there is plenty of scope for anyone wishing to start hybridising in Britain and Europe. Even if the smaller types are very well suited to gardening needs in Britain and Europe, it is important, nonetheless, that each be given its own special situation. Only thus can it be displayed to full effect without being swamped amid a mass of other blooms. Many of these blooms of brilliantly contrasting colour can present difficulties when colour-theming a border but it is always better to use a large block of one variety rather than many different patterned varieties together.

Historic Varieties

Banbury Contrast	(1964 Brummitt)	bicolour with red-brown and orange-yellow segments
Bonanza	(1954 Ferrick)	buff with brown eye-zone
Dixie Land	(1964 Wynne)	large, pink-melon flowers with mahogany-brown eye-zone
Frans Hals FCC	(1955 Flory)	very pretty rust and butter-yellow bicolour flowers
Imperator	(1925 Perry)	rich orange-red with deeper-coloured throat and eye-zone
Lynn Hall	(1958 Hall)	small light pink flowers with wine-red eye, early sort
Mikado	(1929 Stout)	rich orange-red with deeper-coloured throat and eye-zone
Mini Skirt	(1966 Lambert)	small, bitone pink flowers with rosé-coloured eye
Orient	(1965 Wynne)	strong salmon-pink, medium-sized flowers with plum-coloured eye
Painted Lady	(1942 Russell)	orange-brown bicolour, starry flowers on tall stems
Prairie Charmer	(1962 Marsh)	pink-melon-coloured with strong purple-blue eye
Wideyed	(1954 Craig)	light yellow with purple band, evergreen, perfectly winter-hardy

Large-flowered Varieties

Bette Davis Eyes	(1983 Kirchhoff)	lavender-buff, intense purple eye-zone, evergreen
Chinese Temple Flower	(1980 Munson)	clear lilac-lavender, bold purple band above cream-green throat, evergreen, tetraploid
Elizabeth Anne Hudson	(1975 Munson)	purple, peach edge, pink eye, tetraploid
French Porcelain	(1976 Munson)	pale lilac, deep burgundy-red eye, tetraploid
Gay Cravat	(1976 Peck)	pink-melon, wine-red eye, rich green throat, tetraploid
Holiday Delight	(1978 Stevens)	orange, deep red eye, tetraploid
King's Cloak	(1969 Munson)	blend of rosy-pinks, mauve eye, tetraploid
Look Away	(1974 Sellers)	brown, chocolate-brown eye, tetraploid

Paper Butterfly	(1983 Morss)	cream-peach and blue-violet blend, violet eye-zone, green throat, evergreen, tetraploid
Real Wind	(1977 Wild)	pale coral-orange, distinct rose halo, tetraploid
Royal Reflections	(1973 Munson)	bicolour coral-red and yellow, tetraploid
Siloam Double Classic	(1985 Henry)	double rose-pink, darker eye
Siloam Double Rose	(1979 Henry)	brilliant rose-pink, deep red eye-zone

Small-flowered Varieties

Angel Artistry	(1982 Soules)	rose-pink and lavender blend, purple eye-zone
Buffy's Doll	(1969 Williamson)	flesh-pink, wine-red band, yellow-green throat
Corsican Bandit	(1981 Hudson)	flat, round cream with maroon eye-zone
Cosmic Hummingbird	(1979 Kirchhoff)	peach-buff, ruby-red eye-zone, lemon-yellow throat, very early
Little Fruit Cup	(1988 Guidry)	pale peach, strawberry-red eye-zone, green throat
Little Gypsy Vagabond	(1979 Cruse)	creamy-yellow, bold purple-black eye-zone
Little Maggie	(1981 Williamson)	light rose, burgundy-red eye-zone, reblooming, evergreen
Pandora's Box	(1980 Talbott)	pale cream, purple-red eye-zone, green throat
Pyewacket	(1979 Hudson)	ivory-peach-pink, bold plum-red eye-zone
Siloam Bo Peep	(1978 Henry)	orchid-pink, dark purple eye-zone
Siloam Button Box	(1976 Henry)	creamy, circular-shaped flowers, chestnut-brown eye-zone
Siloam French Marble	(1979 Henry)	ivory, cherry-red eye-zone, green throat
Siloam Little Girl	(1976 Henry)	shrimp-pink, rose-pink eye-zone
Siloam Shocker	(1981 Henry)	pink, bright red eye-zone, conspicuous green throat
Siloam Uri Winniford	(1981 Henry)	deep cream, large dark claret eye-zone, ruffled margin
Swapshop	(1978 Warner)	bicolour yellow and mahogany-brown, evergreen
Todd Munroe	(1974 Sholar)	light flesh-pink, fuchsia-red eye-zone

Miniature-flowered Varieties

Bumble Bee	(1964 Williamson)	light-yellow, rose-red eye-zone, low-growing
Fingal's Cave	(1979 Talbott)	purple-lavender blend, near-blue eye-zone
Little Brown Koko	(1976 Croker/Baumann)	brown, purple-brown eye-zone, yellow throat
Little Showoff	(1972 Williamson)	cream-coloured flowers with bright red eye-zone
Little Woman	(1969 Wild)	flesh-coloured flowers with cherry-red eye and green heart
Siloam Fairy Tale	(1978 Henry)	very pale pink with rich orchid-pink pattern
Siloam June Bug	(1978 Henry)	golden flowers with dark chestnut-brown eye
Siloam Tee Tiny	(1981 Henry)	'cattleya-pink' with purple-coloured eye and green throat

American Hemerocallis Society Awards

One might wonder why it is that certain varieties have been included here and others omitted. Drawing up a list of recommendations of this kind always tends to be somewhat subjective, if only because there are so many hybrids that no one can know or assess them all. On the other hand one can make a more objective selection simply by listing those varieties that have won one or more prizes, although not all award winners are suited to European conditions. There are several specific awards given for individual characteristics, for example colour, size or fragrance. The flowers will not be described in this context since most will have been covered in the various colour groups.

The Stout Medal is the highest award of the American Hemerocallis Society. No hybrid that gains this award can be simply a nine-days' wonder, since the plant's introduction must have occurred some years earlier. It is, for instance, a requirement that it should have received the 'Award of Merit' at least three years before; this is a distinction given to no more than ten day lilies in any year. Furthermore the Stout Medal is one of the oldest awards. To date it has been awarded to the following:

1950	Hesperus
1951	Painted Lady
1952	Potentate
1953	Revolute
1954	Dauntless
1955	Prima Donna
1956	Naranja
1957	Ruffled Pinafore

MAKING THE CHOICE

1958	High Noon		1970	Frances Fay, Luxury Lace
1959	Salmon Sheen		1971	Satin Glass
1960	Fairy Wings		1972	Skiatook Cardinal
1961	Playboy		1973	Green Valley
1962	Bess Ross		1974	Winsome Lady
1963	Multnomah		1975	Jest
1964	Frances Fay		1976	Clarence Simon
1965	Luxury Lace		1977	White Formal
1966	Cartwheels		1978	Hope Diamond
1967	Full Reward		1979	Oriental Ruby
1968	Satin Glass		1980	Green Flutter
1969	May Hall		1981	Prester John
1970	Ava Michelle		1982	Raindrop
1971	Renee		1983	Ed Murray
1972	Hortensia		1984	Red Rum
1973	Lavender Flight		1985	Olive Bailey Langdon
1974	Winning Ways		1986	Yesterday's Memories
1975	Clarence Simon		1987	To be announced
1976	Green Flutter		1988	To be announced
1977	Green Glitter		1989	Russian Rhapsody
1978	Mary Todd		1990	To be announced
1979	Moment of Truth		1991	Condilla
1980	Bertie Ferris			
1981	Ed Murray			
1982	Ruffled Apricot			
1983	Sabie			
1984	My Belle			
1985	Stella d'Oro			
1986	Janet Gayle			
1987	Becky Lynn			
1988	Martha Adams			
1989	Brocaded Gown			
1990	Fairy Tale Pink			
1991	Betty Woods			

The **Lenington All-American Award** ranks with the Stout Medal as a mark of distinction, because in order to qualify for the award the hybrid must have been introduced at least ten years previously and, as the title explains, receive votes from all over the US. In other words it means that the plant has proved itself in the cool north of the country as well as in the heat of California.

The **Donn Fischer Memorial Cup** goes to the best miniature variety of the year. Although the term miniature refers to the size of the bloom, the plant itself is small. Clearly such plants are suitable for gardens where space is at a premium.

1962	Golden Chimes
1963	Tinker Bell
1964	Curls
1965	Thumbelina
1966	Lula Mae Purnell
1967	Corky
1968	Bitsy
1969	Lona Eaton Miller
1970	Red Mittens
1971	Toyland
1972	Apricot Angel
1973	Bertie Ferris
1974	Squeaky
1975	Little Grapette

1976	Puddin		1986	Chorus Line
1977	Butterpat		1987	Pandora's Box
1978	Raindrop		1988	Siloam Jim Cooper
1979	Stella d'Oro		1989	Sugar Cookie
1980	Little Celena		1990	Janice Brown
1981	Fox Grape		1991	Enchanter's Spell
1982	Siloam June Bug			
1983	Siloam Red Toy			
1984	Peach Fairy			
1985	Pardon Me			
1986	Little Zinger			
1987	Siloam Tee Tiny			
1988	Yellow Lollipop			
1989	Siloam Bertie Ferris			
1990	Texan Sunlight			
1991	Siloam Grace Stamile			

The **Ida Munson Award** is reserved for the best double flower variety of the year.

1975	Double Cutie
1976	Prester John
1977	Pojo
1978	King Alfred
1979	Peach Soufflé
1980	Double Razzle Dazzle
1981	Double Bourbon
1982	Pa Pa Gulino
1983	Betty Woods
1984	Condilla
1985	Yazoo Soufflé
1986	Siloam Double Rose
1987	Stroke of Midnight
1988	Siloam Double Classic
1989	Rachel My Love
1990	Cabbage Flower
1991	Highland Lord

Just as there is an award for the best miniature bloom, so there is also one for the most outstanding small-flowered hybrid. This is the **Annie T. Giles Award**, which was introduced two years after the previous one.

1964	McPick
1965	Luxury Lace
1966	Melon Balls
1967	Little Rainbow
1968	Renee
1969	Little Wart
1970	Green Flutter
1971	Suzie Wong
1972	Guardian Angel
1973	Bambi Doll
1974	Buffys Doll
1975	Little Business
1976	Ed Murray
1977	Little Infant
1978	Little Greenie
1979	Red Rum
1980	Siloam Purple Plum
1981	Lord Camden
1982	Lullaby Baby
1983	Siloam Bo Peep
1984	Wynnson
1985	Siloam Virginia Henson

From 1974 to 1983, i.e. during the early days of white day lilies, the **Robert P. Miller Memorial Award** was presented annually for the best (almost) white tetraploid variety.

1974	Silver Fan
1975	White Cloud
1976	Olive Langdon
1977	Astolat
1978	Chateau Blanc
1979	Ming Snow
1980	Snowy Apparition
1981	Blanco Real, Soft Caress
1982	Gloria Blanca
1983	Snow Ballerina

MAKING THE CHOICE

The **Richard C. Peck Award** could be gained only once by a plant breeder. It was presented for the best tetraploid hybrid of the year, but was discontinued in 1983.

1974	Mary Todd
1975	King's Cloak
1976	Douglas Dale
1977	Ruffled Apricot
1978	Sombrero Way
1979	Chicago Knobby
1980	Dancing Shiva
1981	Apple Tart
1982	Frozen Jade
1983	Midnight Magic

Meanwhile the latest breeding objective is no longer 'white' but 'blue'. There is therefore now an award for the best lavender or purple-coloured variety of the year and this is called the **James E. Marsh Award**.

1981	Swirling Water
1982	Crown Royal
1983	Sebastian
1984	Siloam Tee Tiny
1985	Royal Heritage
1986	Super Purple
1987	Violet Hour
1988	Hamlet
1989	Graceful Eye
1990	Zinfandel

No explanation should be needed for the **L. Ernest Plouf Consistently Very Fragrant Hemerocallis Award**.

1979	Willard Gardner
1980	Tender Love
1981	Frozen Jade
1982	Siloam Double Rose
1983	Ida Miles
1984	Siloam Mama
1985	Siloam Double Classic
1986	Hudson Valley
1987	Evening Bell
1988	Chorus Line
1989	Golden Scroll
1990	Smoky Mountain Autumn
1991	Siloam Spizz

The **Don Stevens Memorial Award** is the most recent of the prizes. It goes to the most beautiful colour pattern of the year. The variety, therefore, has to have a flower with a band or an eye.

1985	Siloam Double Classic
1986	Bette Davis Eyes
1987	Paper Butterfly
1988	Will Return
1989	Siloam Virginia Henson
1990	Janice Brown
1991	New Series

PROPAGATION AND SELECTION OF HYBRIDS

Pollination and Fertilisation

When one considers how many different day lily hybrids there already are, one might well feel that one has little chance of creating something new. On the other hand, we have probably all seen the day lily whose size, shape, or colour was quite pleasing, but which failed in some other way; perhaps it was not well enough branched or not weather-proof... This is just where the hybridiser comes into his or her own to try to make some slight improvement. Therefore, if the reader has ambitions to try breeding plants, he or she should not simply aim to create a 'true blue', or some other new colour variety, but should also pay heed to the other aspects which were addressed in the chapter entitled 'Modern Hybrids'. In any case the pursuit is one which he or she will undoubtedly find both stimulating and rewarding.

The Parent Plants

The first and perhaps most important rule of hybridising is to take care over the choice of parent plants. From the start one should have a definite objective in mind. Unfortunately there are breeders, and not just in the USA, whose main aim seems to be the introduction of $100 (or even £100) varieties through the simple expedient of crossing two $50 sorts. Such a method is not to be recommended, particularly if the end result fails to show any great improvement. The problem should be approached from a different angle altogether. The parent plants should not merely be beautiful to look at, above all they should be healthy, weather-proof, well-branched, long-flowering and possibly even fragrant. The plants need to have good, firm flowers that open well.

There are of course times when one wishes to make a cross in order to gain a positive quality from a parent despite the latter's defects. First and foremost one must avoid crossing this plant with another that has exactly the same defects. Take for example 'Dance Ballerina Dance'; on no account should this variety be crossed with another that also fails to open well. On the other hand, if there is a characteristic that one wishes to emphasise, let

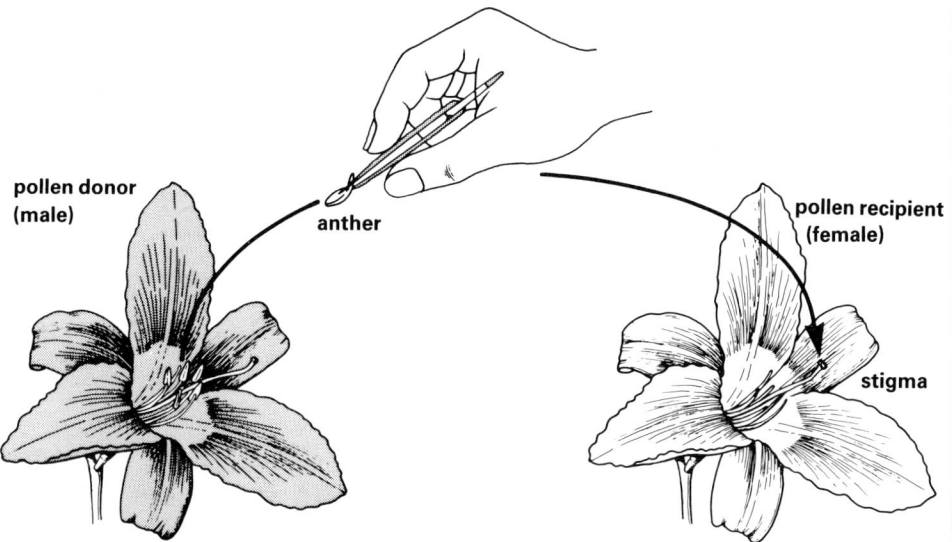

Figure 31 For pollination the pollen from the male parent plant has to be transferred to the stigma of the mother plant, whose anthers have been removed, so as to prevent self-fertilisation.

us say 'ruffling', then one needs to back-cross the hybrid onto one or other of its parents. This is a process known as line breeding. It is important to realise, however, that any inherited faults will tend to become more and more exaggerated. Line breeding if repeated too often leads to weak plants prone to disease. The alternative to in-breeding is out-breeding or out-crossing (i.e. crossing with a plant that is not an immediate relative), introducing new 'blood' into the strain.

The choice of parents thus depends primarily on what one intends to achieve. In this respect one needs to allow oneself to be guided to some extent by intuition, for the raising of a new hybrid is often a matter of luck. In order to avoid confusing beginners, or indeed putting them off altogether, with too many technical terms, special breeding projects will be explained in detail in the next section. It does not really matter whether one works with diploids or tetraploids. The latter generally tend to produce fewer seeds and one also has to reckon with a few losses during germination, but on the other hand their breeding potential is greater in that the proportion of variants is greater despite the smaller actual number of plants raised. Attempts to cross diploids with tetraploids will not be successful at all.

The actual technicalities of hybridising are quite simple. One removes the open anther (pollen sac) of one flower and strokes it against the stigma of another flower, usually that of another variety. It sounds very simple and amateurs have indeed had some startling results this way, though for the professional it is, of course, too simplistic. For this reason let us follow the procedure adopted by a German breeder who has more than 1,000 hybrids to his credit. Early in the morning, at around four o'clock, he goes on his first rounds removing the anthers, still closed at this stage, from the designated pollen parents. The anthers are placed in shallow containers in such a way that the air can get at them to dry them. In a short while they burst and the powdery yellow pollen spills out. The anthers have also been removed from the seed parents and destroyed if surplus to requirements; this measure prevents self-pollination.

Even from the pollen experts can tell whether the pollen parent is fertile or not. Only loose, golden-yellow pollen dust will lead to germination; hard and infertile pollen is white. The fertility of the seed parent can only be established definitely by trial and error. Early morning, especially if it is still cool, is the best time for pollinating tetraploids. It is sometimes possible to tell if the stigma is ready for pollination by the fact that it may exude a sticky liquid. Diploid varieties can be pollinated successfully up to midday, but the success rate decreases towards evening. Particularly hot days are not ideal for pollination and long rainy periods can also have an adverse effect on the ripening of seeds. However, one should not allow oneself to be put off by this – 'Katrinchen' (only 30cm high and an unregistered variety from a German breeder, Fritz Koehlein) resisted my crossing attempts for two years; then in the third year, without my having to lift a finger, it suddenly produced seeds all on its own. Success in the field of hybridising depends not simply on the determination of the hybridiser – chance also seems to play a not unimportant part.

Pollen Storage

It sometimes happens that the male parent is in bloom while the female is still only in bud, but storing the pollen presents no problem. If the expected delay is no more than a matter of keeping the pollen until the evening, or the following morning, the pollen containers can simply be placed in the refrigerator. An empty eggbox makes an ideal receptacle. If the pollen is to be kept for a longer time or even sent by post to another hybridiser, rather more care is needed. The pollen has to be scraped out of the pollen sacs very carefully, making sure that no fleshy pieces of the anther are included, since these cause decay. Gelatine capsules, of the kind used for medicine and which dissolve in the stomach, make excellent little storage vessels. Some tubes of pills (or, for example, 'Diastix', used for diabetic urine analysis) contain tiny sachets of silica gel, which has the property of absorbing moisture from the air. Put the capsules in the pill tube, but do not seal it, and then place this, together with the silica gel, in a sealed container in the refrigerator. Kept cool and dry like this the pollen will remain viable for several weeks.

When the time comes for using the pollen that has been stored thus, one puts the capsules into something like the above-mentioned eggbox, making sure that while working in the garden one keeps it shaded, so as to prevent the pollen from drying out. All that is then necessary for the act of pollination is to open the capsule and dip the stigma, the top third of the pistil, into the pollen. Some people prefer the brush method, in which the pollen is applied to the stigma by means of a small paintbrush, but the problem with this is that the brush needs to be very carefully cleaned after the application of one kind of pollen and before the next; since this is well-nigh impossible, the hybridising carries an element of risk. A pair of tweezers, on the other hand, will be invaluable. Some people go so far as to cover the stigma with a small foil cap (foil from a bar of chocolate is suitable) in order to make absolutely certain that no chance pollination can occur, but since the flowers close again at night in any case, chance pollination is a most unlikely event.

Labelling

It is essential to keep detailed records of all hybridising work. There are several ways in which this can be done. It is not always necessary to keep a record book, but it is absolutely essential to use small tie-on labels. Nor is it enough merely to mark each plant, since each of its blooms may have been crossed with a different plant. On the label one can write a reference number and details as to parentage and so on, and these details can then be entered in the record book. Alternatively, if the labels themselves are big enough, the names of the parent plants can be written directly on this in addition to the date and so on. The conventional way of recording the data is as follows: first the name of the mother plant, i.e. the plant from which the seeds will be harvested, followed by the name of the pollen donor; one should also put down the date of pollination, the date when the pollen was collected (if this is not the same) and possibly the sequence number of the particular trial. Thus an entry could read

'85/145 31/07/85 "Lusty Lealand" × "Galena Holiday"'

One should not feel too disappointed if, despite all one's efforts, the plants fail to set seed. *Pollination* and *fertilisation* are two different things. The act of pollination can be carried out in the manner described above. Whether this leads to fertilisation is quite another matter and depends on a number of factors. Prevailing weather conditions clearly play an important part. Also of importance is the state of the female gametes, the ovules, in the ovary; sometimes they are simply not properly developed. When the pollen grain has settled on the stigma it begins to develop a pollen tube that grows down through the style and allows the male gametes to pass through into the ovary. The fusion of the male and the female cells is the process known as fertilisation. Only after fertilisation can the seed begin to develop. In a few days the flower segments will fall off and the ovary will begin to swell. It goes without saying that plants used for breeding should on no account be dead-headed! As a rule 40 per cent of the flowers that are pollinated develop into mature seed capsules.

It is not difficult from now on to follow the development of the seed capsules, that is if the weather does not decide to play tricks. If the capsules start to wrinkle as a result of unfavourable weather conditions, one may be sure that the seeds will not come to anything. If all has gone well, after between 60 and 80 days the capsules will have turned brown. The seeds should now be ripe and ready for harvest. We shall now digress a little for the benefit of those who might wish to delve more deeply into some of the technical aspects of day lily hybridisation.

Special Breeding Projects

If you already have some experience in the raising of new hybrids, you may sooner or later wish to specialise. An area that might appeal could be that of tetraploids, perhaps even working with colchicine. Or one could experiment with winter-hardy evergreen varieties, or concentrate on particular flower shapes and/or colours. Whatever direction one takes, one or other of the specialist sections of the American Hemerocallis Society could prove immensely helpful and membership of the AHS is therefore essential. The members of these specialist sections keep in touch with each other through correspondence, and a series of 'round robins' that encourage the exchange of ideas and information between members in Europe, Australia and the USA.

Relevant addresses may be found in the AHS News Sheets, or can be obtained from the Foreign Members' Secretary. The following are some of the 38 round robins one could join:

Blue One
Double Crossers
European Robin
Everblooming
Evergreen
First Dwarf and Mini
First Tetraploid
First Fragrance
Intrepid (hardy varieties)
Mini and Small-flowered
Species
Spider
Tetrobin
True Blue

We shall examine briefly just three possible avenues of future hybridising: small varieties, which are important for small gardens, and the development of both white and blue varieties. We shall begin with the 'minis', which are a great talking point at the moment, particularly since Pauline Henry's 'Siloam' varieties began to dominate the trade and popularity lists. There are three main objectives in the breeding of miniature varieties: new and unusual colours, small blooms and short scapes. It has already been pointed out that the size of the flower and the length of the scape should be in proportion. And if one does not pay enough attention to the colour and pattern effects of the flowers one is raising, they may scarcely differ at all from chance seedlings. It is therefore necessary to develop a breeding programme based on the choice of correct parent plants. Not every variety that is currently popular is fertile, though, of course, its parents must have been. It pays to consult the checklist to find out the hybrid's origin, so as to avoid simply replicating a breeding programme someone else has already pursued. On the other hand there is no need to be afraid of copyright infringement, because any seedlings produced are bound to be different from previous ones, as one occasionally finds with plants that are said to be sibling varieties. Time and time again research into the genealogy of a given mini variety brings us back to *H. minor*; almost all minis will have been recrossed one or more times with this species. There is no harm, therefore, in giving the latter space in one's garden. More will be said about the actual selection of seedlings later.

It is a much more difficult matter to strive for certain definite colours, especially if these are as far removed from the natural colour range of the species as are white and blue. The problem, therefore, has to be tackled scientifically, by studying the colour pigments present in the flowers. This is not as formidable as it may seem. The pigments are:

Carotenoids
carotene (carotin)	orange
lycopene	orange-red

Anthocyanidins
cyanidin	red
delphidin	purple-red, blue
malvidin	purple-red, blue
pelargonidin	salmon (orangey)
paeonidin	red

Flavones and Flavonols
(co-pigments)
agipenin	cream
kaempferol	ivory, cream
luteolin	yellowish
myricetin	cream
quercetin	cream

From the plant breeder's point of view, the most important pigments are the *flavones*. On their own they have little colour and would yield simply white, cream, ivory, pale yellow and pale orange. A clue as to their true nature lies in the fact that they are called *co-pigments*, for they almost invariably occur in combination with other pigments, usually one of the *anthocyanidins*. The two pigment groups are related and have crystal structures similar to that of sugar. Above all the *anthocyanidins* tend to be intensified by *flavones* and occasionally their colour effect is also altered. An excess of *flavones* has an additional effect: since there is now too much pigment for all of it to dissolve, the excess crystallises out and manifests itself as 'diamond dusting'. Thus when one is making the choice of suitable parent plants, one can be sure that one that has this glittering effect must contain a high proportion of *flavones*.

For a time it was thought that one could produce a white day lily more quickly by using tetraploids. From 1974 to 1983 the AHS donated a separate trophy for 'the best white tetraploid variety'. The theory is that the same amount of sap, together with the dissolved pigments, would be spread over the greater surface area of tetraploid flowers. In other words, if the pigmented components of a light colour are also diluted, i.e. more widely dispersed, they would appear paler and paler, maybe even practically white. Although the idea might sound fairly simple, its efficacy has so far been neither proved nor disproved. Doubling the chromosome content may also lead to an increase in the content of secondary substances, as was found with medicinal plants. In practice it should not make too much difference whether one uses diploids or tetraploids to try to produce a white day lily. The dedicated breeder will try both types.

Up to now almost all white varieties that have come on to the market still have a tinge of ivory, yellow or pink in them. They all still contain *carotenoids*, which produce yellow, orange or red hues. Only if these can be entirely eliminated will we get a genuine pure white. The problem is that the ability of the varieties to retain *carotenoids* remains dominant when crossed. The search is on, therefore, to find varieties containing a so-far-unknown pigment that will neutralise *carotenoids*. For the moment this pigment has been named *anti-carotenoid*. M. Kasha is fairly certain that there are day lilies that contain such a substance. Although these day lilies are themselves by no means white, they nevertheless contain this so-called 'white factor'. This has been shown to exist in:

'Blue Bristol'	= lavender-blue
'Catherine Woodbery'	= lavender-pink
'Color Splash'	= strong rosé
'Shadrach'	= lavender
'Pony'	= lavender and cream

Similarly one can list those hybrids that have a high flavonol content. It is also possible to list those varieties that, as the reader will see later, can also be used to propagate blue varieties. Almost-white hybrids that would make suitable crossing partners are:

'Acadiana Snow'
'Call to Remembrance'
'Chosen One'
'First Snow'
'Ice Carnival'
'Julia Tanner'
'Moment of Truth'
'Quixotic'
'Sally Lake'
'Ski Chalet'
'Snowfall'
'White Wings'

Admittedly some of the hybrids in this list have light colours that result not so much from the actual colour of the pigment, as from their ability to absorb ultra-violet radiation. If the breeding objective is 'white', then it is immaterial by which route one achieves it. This is not so in the case of 'blue' for, assuming that the same colour change takes place with day lilies as can be observed with vetches, the co-pigment will shift the colour effect from red to mauve, or from purple to blue. The diagram should help to clarify the changes.

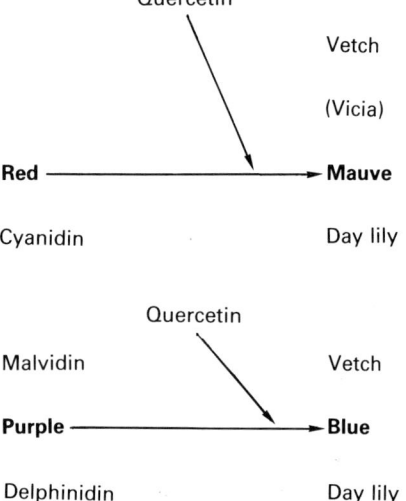

It would therefore seem (in theory at any rate) that one needs simply to cross a variety containing a high proportion of delphinidin with a white variety to obtain a 'blue'. But of course theory is one thing, and practice quite another. It is interesting to note that 'pure whites' do not promise more chance of success, since they owe their whiteness to their ability to absorb UV radiation and so for our purposes cream-coloured varieties with their high quercetin content are more suitable. Hybrids of this kind are:

'Celestial Light'
'Creamy Egret'
'Family Portrait'
'Frivolous Frills'
'So Lovely'

For the other parent one now needs a variety with a high blue, i.e. delphinidin, content. If the proportion of red or cyanidin predominates, then one obtains more mauvey-coloured varieties. The proportion of delphinidin to cyanidin in various hybrids is as follows:

Variety	D:C
'Cajun Caprice'	100:0
'Dawn Delight'	100:0
'Marsh Pixie'	100:0
'Phoenician Wealth'	100:0
'Age of Chivalry'	85:15
'Chicago Royal'	85:15
'Purple Bounty'	75:25
'Quiet Stars'	60:40
'Purple Robe'	50:50
'Tovarich'	40:60
'Liberty'	15:85

Certainly the breeding projects suggested in this section are not particularly easy to realise. On the other hand they do offer the greatest opportunity to achieve something entirely new and, apart from general recognition of one's work, it is also possible to earn some financial reward. One needs only to glance through the lists offering for sale new varieties in the above categories, to see that these can command fairly high prices. However, one might sometimes ask oneself, particularly in the realm of 'blue' varieties, if they are indeed worth the money.

Cultivation and Selection of Plants

Even if one does not intend to go in for hybridising it is desirable to harvest the seed capsules from the individual scapes before they burst open. It is not hard to imagine what would happen if the seeds were scattered immediately around the parent plant. A host of seedlings would grow up that would subsequently prove well-nigh impossible to separate from the parent, but they would not be identical with it. It is therefore best to check the seed capsules regularly to note their state of ripeness. As soon as they have become completely brown they should be removed from the plant and allowed to dry off; in a short while the capsules will burst. Should this happen while the capsule is still on the plant, there should be no delay in collecting the seed.

Almost any type of container, provided that it is not airtight, can be used for storing the seeds or seed capsules. However, one should not simply throw them all into the same pot, for it will prove extremely difficult later on, if not impossible, to recognise which came from which crossing. My own choice for storing seeds is envelopes; they are easy to write on and do not take up much room. If the seeds are not to be sown fairly soon, they may be stored in a refrigerator, though they will tend to lose moisture. But it does not matter too much if they have shrivelled a little by the time spring comes, because all one has to do is to soak them in water for one or two days prior to sowing.

It is, of course, perfectly reasonable to want to see results as soon as possible. For this reason it often pays to sow the seeds immediately upon collection, so that by the following spring one already has plantable seedlings. Clearly, sowing out of doors is out of the question. So how does one tackle the problem if one does not have a greenhouse or a frame available? Seed boxes may be put on a well-lit window ledge where between December and January the seeds will germinate in a temperature of about 5°C. If such seedlings are then planted out in May, they grow into robust plants that will generally come into flower in their second year.

If one obtains one's seeds from exchanges or even from the USA (the choice of *Hemerocallis* seeds available through the trade tends to be rather limited), one will have noticed that sometimes the seeds seem to lie dormant for quite a while before they begin to germinate. There is, however, a way of accelerating the germination process, though before embarking on it one needs to consider whether one has sufficient space. It involves cutting the seeds; this is a frequent practice with hard-shelled seeds such as those of irises, where one frequently has to wait much longer for germination. Usually there is no such trouble with *Hemerocallis*, but as these respond remarkably well to the treatment, it is described below.

A close look at the seed grains will reveal that they are not uniformly round or ovoid, but that there is a slight bump at the point where the germ lies concealed, though this will be more difficult to detect if the seed has become dehydrated, for then additional irregularities will also be present. If this is the case, place the seeds in some water in a glass (or a test tube) for three or four days. It is important to change the water every day. At first the seeds will float to the surface, but gradually, as they become saturated, more of them will sink. They are now ready for cutting.

A razor blade or scalpel will be needed for the operation, as well as a weak disinfectant solution such as Milton, a pair of tweezers and several preserving jars (Kilner or similar). First of all everything likely to come into contact with the specimens must be cleaned with disinfectant: not only tools, but hands and containers also. Then take one of the seeds and hold it with the tweezers in such a way that the bump containing the germ can be carefully cut off with the blade. The black skin should not be removed beforehand. The tiny round white embryo should be visible, surrounded by the ivory-coloured nutrient tissue. Having put some vermiculite, perlite or simply moistened peat into the lid of the preserving jar, place the prepared seeds, cut surface uppermost, on it. It should be possible to position all the seeds from one capsule slightly apart from each other on the one lid. Next the jar is inverted and placed over the lid; in this way the seeds are in a constant moisture-laden atmosphere.

The preserving jars should then be transferred to a warm place, which does not need to be light, at least not until the seeds have sent out their first plumule. Normally this process takes one or two weeks, but, once the plumules have developed, sunlight is needed. Seeds that, despite the precautions, start to become mouldy should be removed with tweezers without delay before they infect others. When the seedlings reach a height of 2–3cm, they should be pricked out into small plastic pots filled with normal potting compost. There is no need to worry about picking the seedlings up with the tweezers; holding them by the remaining nutrient tissue is unlikely to damage them. They usually lift easily out of the germinating medium. If the seedlings are grown on in a heated propagating cloche or frame, they may well flower in the year following the seed collection.

By whatever method one sets about rearing one's seedlings, they will probably be in some kind of seed tray or pot initially. Although *Hemerocallis* will normally withstand frost, seedlings should not be planted out until May, since weather conditions at that time of the year favour a really vigorous surge in growth. From then until the appearance of the first bloom there is really not much else to be done, apart from keeping the young plants free from weeds and watching for any possible pests. Feeding the plants is dealt with in the chapter entitled 'Cultivation of Day Lilies', p. 120; suffice it to say here that for the first two years it is probably better to use compost. Mulching also seems to be effective, but again this will be dealt with in greater detail in a later section.

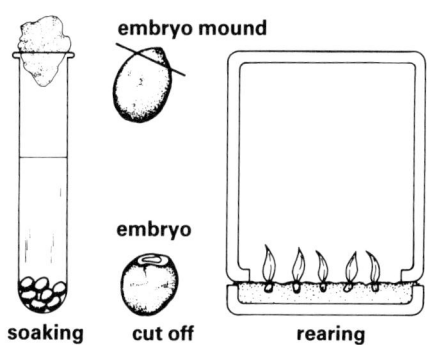

Figure 32 Germination can be hastened by means of the abscission method.

Selection and Registration

It's all been more or less plain sailing so far, but now comes the tricky bit! One has by now anything from 100 to 500 seedlings, all in flower. Not all of them will be better than their parents. Indeed some will be so ugly that they should be discarded forthwith. A few will be quite pleasing, and the next step is to divide these into two groups.

At most 2–5 per cent of the seedlings will be good enough to register. Often none are good enough. A further 10 per cent will be suitable for further hybridisation.

With luck there might be an absolute winner among them.

However, on no account should one pass a firm judgement in the first year or put a variety forward for registration. A variety needs to flower really well for three successive years before one even considers this step, and one should not allow one's natural enthusiasm to blind one to other aspects of the plant's performance: the branching of the scape, the length of time that the flower remains open and whether the foliage is healthy, to name but a few.

One also needs to decide which, if any, of one's hybrids are worth propagating. One way is to invite people from whom one might expect an honest and worthwhile opinion to give just that. Eventually, however, it comes down to one's own choice.

In Britain there is official recognition for newly-introduced plants of merit. They may be put up for awards given by the Royal Horticultural Society in several different ways. Individual blooms may be entered for award at the Summer Flower Show and the Society's Halls at Westminster. There are also on-going trials for *Hemerocallis* at the Society's garden at Wisley in Surrey, and breeders and nurserymen may enter their plants in the autumn. The plants are grown on and assessed for at least three years and may be given an FCC (First Class Certificate) or AM (Award of Merit) or PC (Preliminary Commendation). Further details are available from the Trials Officer at Wisley. This scheme is open to growers all over the world, not just from the UK, and a list of past award winners is available from Wisley. The FCC or AM are usually added after the plant's name in nursery catalogues (as are the American Hemerocallis Society's awards). The awards are given only to those plants that have been registered. It is a pity that more British and European varieties are not entered. These are too often overlooked in favour of apparently more exotic imports.

There are three evaluation centres or trial grounds in West Germany. The reasons for having three of them are, firstly, so as to obtain the opinions of three independent judges, and, secondly, to grow the plants in areas with different climatic conditions.

To give some idea of what is entailed in such an assessment of merit, let us look at the marking scheme used in the three German Trial Grounds for two-year-old plants, remembering that only those seedlings that gain 60 points go through to the final scrutiny in the third year (see table).

Where registration comes in useful is if, for example, one obtains a plant through exchange and all one knows about it is its name. If the plant is registered one should be able to ascertain the height to which it grows, the size of its flowers and so on. There are growers who may not send their hybrids for registration, but they will use a certain distinctive prefix, which indicates its origin.

Registration is not all that complicated and in Britain all that a raiser has to do is to apply to the Registrar of the British Hosta and Hemerocallis Society who will make the neces-

Evaluation of Second-year Hybrids	
Criterion	Max. Points
Flower shape (normal weather)	20
Colour, categorised as follows	
• yellow, orange, melon, brownish	10
• red, pink-red, purple, blended	15
• white, black, pink, lavender, violet, eyed, edged	20
Structure of whole plant (harmony)	15
Abundance of flowers (compared with ranks)	10
Reproductive ability	8
Florescence	8
Duration of flower opening	6
Durability of open flower	7
Influence of cold weather conditions	15

sary arrangements. The conventional terms and abbreviations that need to be used in the description are all explained in the chapter entitled 'Modern Hybrids'. Once an entry has been registered its name is protected, which means that that particular hybrid cannot be marketed under any other name, nor can the chosen name be used by anyone else for another hybrid. There is, of course, some cost to all this.

The naming should not be haphazard, and one or two rules have to be observed. Needless to say one cannot use a name that has already been allocated. Nor is one allowed simply to modify an existing name or transpose the wording (for instance, changing 'Ruffled Apricot' to 'Apricot Ruffles'). The name may consist of two words, but must not exceed three; titles such as 'Mr', 'Mrs' and 'Dr' should be omitted and, if the name of a living person is to be used, permission should always be sought beforehand. Naming a flower after oneself is frowned upon, and Latinised names are definitely not allowed, since such nomenclature is reserved purely for species. Moreover, should one find oneself in the fortunate position of being given a beautiful new seedling by a friend, one should certainly not attempt to get it registered without that friend's full permission.

Hemerocallis Raised in Europe

Many modern American day lilies are exceedingly expensive, especially as they may not even perform well in Europe. By comparison hybrids of European origin are more moderately priced. The European (including British) hybrids may be fewer in number, but they are of a very high standard and able to hold their own against international competition. Since the total number of European registrations is not large, we list them all. The list would be even more comprehensive were we to include all unregistered hybrids as well. The pros and cons of registration have already been mentioned and the absence of this or that variety from the list below is not a reflection on its quality, but merely reflects its absence from the International Day Lily Register.

Because the early European

growers, such as Max Steiger, tended not to register their hybrids, the first entry is comparatively recent. Thus, from 1979 to 1986 a total of 46 were registered. These are shown below: (E = early, M = mid-season, L = late).

'Apollo 17' (1983 Reinermann) 55cm, M, 15cm, large yellow flowers with light median stripe, green throat.

'Bayreuther Phoenix' (1981 Koehlein) 65cm, E, 14cm, strong carmine-pink flowers with egg-yolk yellow throat.

'Berggarten' (1985 Moos) 65cm, M, 12cm, mid-pink flowers with white midrib, salmon-pink heart.

'Berlin Circle' (1986 Tamberg) 60cm, M, 15cm, strong melon-coloured flowers, very broad segments, tetraploid.

'Berlin Giant' (1983 Tamberg) 80cm, M, 15cm, strong but light yellow flowers with green throat, tetraploid.

'Berlin Lavender' (1983 Tamberg) 80cm, L, 13cm, lilac flowers with light yellow throat, tetraploid.

'Berlin Multi' (1986 Tamberg) 140cm, M-L, 10cm, small-flowered, maize-yellow variety with very many buds.

'Berlin Oxblood' (1983 Tamberg) 90cm, M, 15cm, deep oxblood-red flowers with small yellow throat, tetraploid.

'Berlin Red' (1983 Tamberg) 75cm, M, 15cm, very weather resistant, radiant red variety, tetraploid.

'Berlin Red Star' (1986 Tamberg) 75cm, M-L, 14cm, flat star-shaped flowers, medium dark red in colour, tetraploid.

'Berlin Red Velvet' (1986 Tamberg) 70cm, M-L, broad segments, velvety deep red in colour, tetraploid.

'Berlin Watermelon' (1979 Tamberg) 70cm, M, 15cm, watermelon-coloured flowers with pale lilac flush, tetraploid.

'Berliner Anfang' (1980 Heimann) 80cm, M, 10cm, well-branched orange-yellow tetraploid.

'Berliner Mondlicht' (1981 Tamberg) 60cm, M, 12cm, light green-yellow flowers, reblooms well, tetraploid.

'Berliner Premiere' (1979 Tamberg) 60cm, E-ML, 13cm, extended blooming, radiant orange-yellow, tetraploid.

'Berliner Zimtstaub' (1983 Tamberg) 90cm, M, 14cm, orange-yellow flowers with red-brown flush, tetraploid.

'Brunhild' (1981 Koehlein) 70cm, M-L, 14cm, tile-red with star-shaped throat, tetraploid.

'Elfriede' (1981 Koehlein) 75cm, E, 14cm, blended cream, pink, melon, tetraploid.

'Georg Rodewald' (1979 Tamberg) 80cm, M, 14cm, orange-yellow star-shaped flowers, tetraploid.

'Gold Frenzy' ('Goldrausch', 1981 Berlin) 65cm, M, 12cm, elegant strong gold-yellow flowers, tetraploid.

'Goldmarie' (1981 Koehlein) 75cm, E, 16cm, giant strong yellow flowers, substantial.

'Grosse Zitrone' (1981 Berlin) 60cm, E-M, 13cm, light yellow variety, tetraploid with colchicine.

'Hannover Start' (1985 Moos) 65cm, M, 16cm, velvety russet flower with golden-yellow midrib.

'Heiteres Rot' (1981 Berlin) 80cm, M, 14cm, elegant medium red flowers, weather-proof, tetraploid.

'Helle Berlinerin' (1981 Tamberg) 70cm, M, 14cm, almost white variety with orange throat, tetraploid.

'Hexenritt' (1981 Berlin) 80cm, M, 15cm, extremely weather-proof, large brilliant red flowers, tetraploid.

'Josef Reinermann' (1985 Reinermann) 85cm, M, 13cm, lavender-purple-coloured with creamy median stripe, tetraploid.

'Kaete Waechter' (1983 Tamberg) 70cm, M, 15cm, dark, pink-lilac flowers, tetraploid.

'Melonencocktail' (1981 Koehlein) 90cm, M-L, 13cm, clear melon colour with small olive-green throat.

'Natzohm' (1983 Reinermann) 55cm, M, 15cm, lemon-yellow, slightly ruffled flowers with green throat.

'Orange Ufo' (1986 Tamberg) 65cm, EM-ML, 14cm, orange-yellow, very wide segments, tetraploid.

'Pfennigparade' (1981 Koehlein) 90cm, E, 7cm, tile-red flowers with orange throat and light edges.

'Pink Ufo' (1986 Tamberg) 90cm, M, 13cm, salmon-pink flowers with darker throat, reblooming tetraploid.

'Rosennymphe' (1981 Koehlein) 65cm, E, 13cm, flowers of cream, pink and melon blend, tetraploid.

'Roter Stammbaum' (1980 Tamberg) 90cm, M-L, 12cm, velvety dark red flowers on tall scapes, tetraploid.

'Rudolf Seyer' (1984 Reinermann) 65cm, M, 10cm, velvety red with darker eye and green throat.

'Rundblick' (1979 Tamberg) 140cm, M-L, 8cm, light yellow with brown patterning on back, tetraploid.

'Schoeppinger Anfang' (1983 Reinermann) 60cm, M, 10cm, light purple with darker eye and large yellow-green throat.

'Schoeppinger Postillon' (1985 Reinermann) 60cm, M, 16cm, very ruffled, golden-yellow flower with green throat.

'Sonnenbarke' (1981 Koehlein) 85cm, M-L, 15cm, yellow-melon-coloured variety with mother-of-pearl sheen, tetraploid.

'Spinne in Lachs' (1986 Tamberg) 100cm, M, 15cm, lavender-pink spider with light orange throat, tetraploid.

'Waltraud Kroeger' (1983 Reinermann) 60cm, M, 15cm, orange-red with darker eye and yellow-green centre, tetraploid.

'Westerwaelder Nordlicht' (1983 Hintze) 70cm, M-L, 17cm, giant strong golden-yellow flower, tetraploid.

'Young CHA' (1986 Tamberg) 90cm, M, 11cm, medium-sized light melon-coloured flowers, tetraploid.

'Zarte Wolke' (1981 Berlin) 85cm, M, 14cm, salmon-pink flowers with halo, tetraploid.

'Zitronenriese' (1986 Tamberg) 90cm, E-M, 16cm, large flowers of light lemon-yellow colour, tetraploid.
Two Belgian varieties are:
'Rouqueffeuil' (1985 van Mulders) 40cm, M, 12cm, strong wine-red with green throat, evergreen.

'Wine Spoon' (1985 van Mulders) 50cm, M, 10cm, violet blend variety with small green throat.

German Awards

In the Federal Republic of Germany there are in all five distinct categories based on the results of the evaluations described earlier. This all stems from a proposal of fairly recent date, 1983 in fact, and is therefore still developing. Since an evaluation in the first growth year is not really worthwhile (subsequent results may well differ considerably), the plants are judged in their second year and again in their third. The plant with the highest number of points of the first evaluation is awarded the **Berlin Trophy**, and the winner in the final evaluation receives the **Karl Foerster Medal**. In addition there are also three **Palmengarten Medals** for the best entries from Frankfurt, which has become the European headquarters for day lily growers.

There is yet another, albeit unofficial, evaluation for new varieties, indeed, one that might prove the most rewarding. Each year day lily growers from all over Germany, from Austria, Belgium and Switzerland send in their choice of the most popular varieties to the headquarters in Frankfurt, and from the names submitted a list of 'The Most Beautiful and Best *Hemerocallis* of Central Europe' is compiled. Because of the international nature of this compilation, which includes American as well as European varieties, any breeder who reaches the first 50 can be justifiably proud. However, since the popularity of a hybrid depends also to some extent on how widely it is distributed, the older and well-proven sorts tend to predominate.

Day lilies are not only suitable for borders, as shown here, but some are suitable for lightly wooded areas, rose beds and edging ponds, binding sloping sites, landscaping civic and municipal areas and public parks.

Hemerocallis exaltata

H. dumortieri

H. forrestii 'Perry's Variety'

H. lilioasphodelus

H. fulva 'Europa'

H. fulva 'Kwanzo'

Hemerocallis species

'Sunstar' (Lester, 1954 USA)

'Golden Chimes' (Fischer, 1954 USA)

'Green Puff' (Spalding, 1977 USA)

'Double Glitter' (Krupien, 1976 USA)

'Frans Hals' (Flory, 1955 USA)

'Osage Delight' (McKeithan, 1954 USA)

Yellow *Hemerocallis* varieties

'Christmas Carol' (Wild, 1971 USA)

'Red Roque' (McKinney, 1977 USA)

'Margaret Marlatt' (Lambert, 1968 USA)

'Spanish Brocade' (Allgood, 1973 USA)

'Bess Ross' (Claar, 1951 USA)

'Willie Bill' (Williamson, 1971 USA)

Red *Hemerocallis* varieties

VEGETATIVE PROPAGATION

Dividing the Root

In the previous section we explained how to propagate day lilies from seed. However, simply raising the seedling of a named variety will not produce more of that variety. The seedlings will be similar but not identical. If a particular named sort is to be marketed, then it must be increased vegetatively. This is a common method of propagating and most gardeners will be familiar with it. The explanations that follow are intended to clarify one or two specific points.

There are very few gardens in which the soil is such that it is possible simply to dig up day lilies and shake the earth from the roots. More often than not one has to dig out the whole plant in order to divide it into separate fans. If one tries to separate single fans from a plant in the ground, one usually finishes up with a damaged fan.

It is always better to dig out clumps completely. If all the soil cannot be removed by shaking alone, it needs to be washed off. With large clumps it is best, having dug them out, to leave them to dry out for a day in a shaded place. This helps to loosen the soil for easier removal, and the plant will not suffer from drying. Then, when the roots are exposed, it is much easier to see exactly where to use the knife, though it is better still if the roots can be simply teased apart.

Unfortunately there are some varieties, such as 'Fashion Delight', in which the fans are very tightly packed; in this case using a knife is unavoidable. It is best to cut vertically downwards so that each part has its root section. But one cannot simply replant this as it is, for in the root tangle there will be many pieces of root that do not belong to this particular fan of foliage. These bits will probably begin to rot, which in itself does not matter, but if the plant has already sustained other damage, then the rot may spread to the wound and so lead to the loss of the entire plant. Hence it is best to remove any loose bits of root that do not belong to the plantlet.

Equally there is no point in trying to plant any pieces of root, because without a crown they cannot grow. Young plants establish themselves

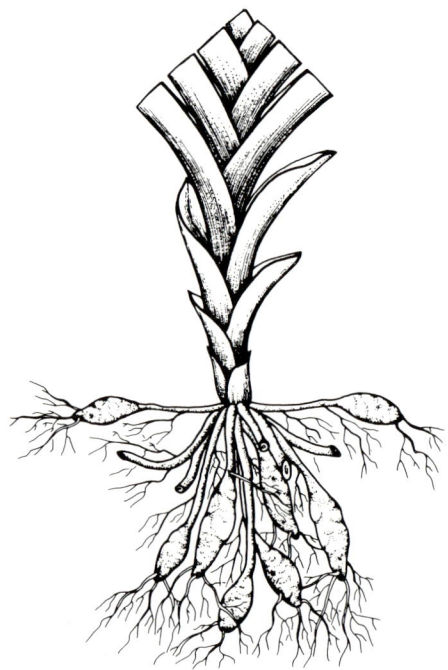

Figure 33 After separation the foliage should be trimmed into a fan shape.

bags. If one receives plants from the USA, one should not be surprised if they arrive loose in the box; if they are at all dry, they should be soaked for a few hours.

Dividing the Crown

People often try to bulk up new varieties so as to obtain as many plants as possible in the shortest time and, before the discovery of the methods discussed below, they tried to achieve this by division of the crown. Needless to say this is a risky business. There are two ways to divide a day lily crown. One is to make a longitudinal section, the other a cross-section. If one is really keen to try these methods, it is best not to use a special plant for the experiment. Unfortunately some losses are inevitable.

Professor F. Kurzmann (1975) described how to carry out a longitudinal section so that each part retained roots. But he added: 'After that it is simply a question of a race between the growth of the day lily on the one hand and that of mould and decay fungi at the cut surfaces on the other. If one first allows the wound to dry off too much, the day lily suffers – if one plants immediately, the causes of decay reproduce more rapidly than a callus can form.'

The next method is likely to be more successful, but it does presuppose that at least two layers of roots emanate from the base. The section through the crown is now made horizontally so that one obtains on the one hand a normal fan of leaves and on the other the lower part without any leaves. The latter

more quickly if the leaves are cut off, reducing the fan to about one-third of its original size. This is worth doing, even if the plants are only to be replanted in one's own garden. It prevents excessive loss of moisture through the leaves while the plant is becoming established.

If one is sending plants through the post, the roots may also need to be cut back to fit into the package. If the plants are to be sent while still in leaf, the roots should be put into a plastic bag, but the top left out so that the leaves may continue to breathe. If the plants are completely dormant, then they are best washed, wrapped in newspaper, which will retain the moisture, and then put into plastic

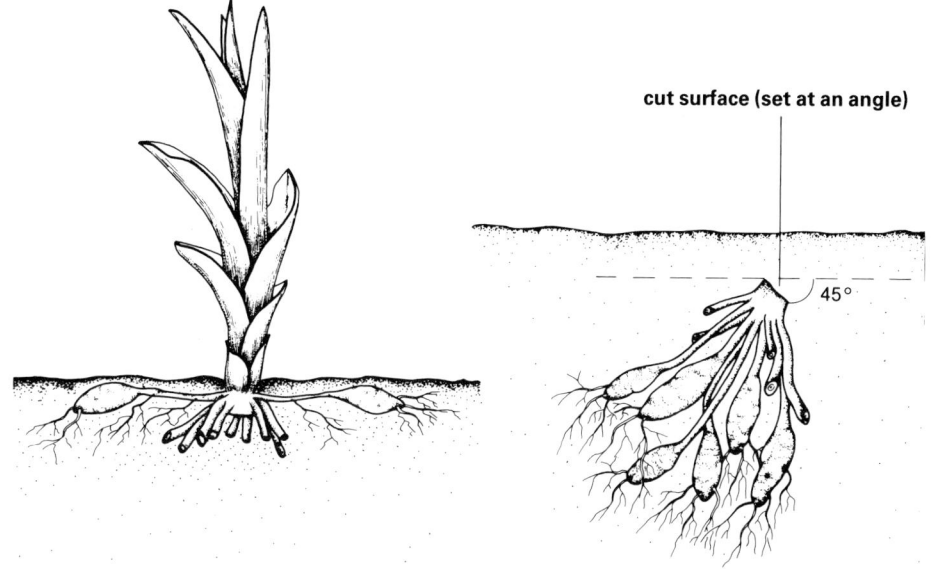

Figure 34 A cross-section of the crown can succeed only if the attached root system is well developed.

part will need special attention in so far as the cut surface has to be dusted with a fungicide and the piece has to be planted at an angle (say 45°) so that any rainwater that penetrates the ground will run off; in this way the crown does not stay too moist.

Here again rot is possible and therefore the plant needs to be dug out once more as soon as the first shoots show. These are then removed from the root stump and replanted separately. C.M. Pittard commented on the process in 1983, saying: 'This method is nerve-racking, especially when one is trying it on a $50 or $100 specimen.' Luckily better methods have since come to hand.

Proliferations

It has already been mentioned that the scapes of day lilies have bracts. Sometimes scapes develop what look like small fans of leaves. These are tiny plantlets in their own right, known as proliferations. If these become rather too big, or cause the scape to bend at this point, they may well detract from the appearance of the plant, but nevertheless such proliferations do present an easy means of propagation.

In the above method one needs only to break the shoot from the scape. If the weather has been sultry, tiny roots may even have developed. All that then remains is to plant the shoot in a pot and invert a glass jar

Figure 35 Proliferations should be pushed into the soil together with the portion of the scape to which they are attached.

in. After the plant had been dug out, the mushy leaves removed and the crown cleansed of all infected matter (see description p. 113), it was replanted. Although I was not all that hopeful, the remainder of the crown managed to produce not just one new fan of leaves but three. Even though these were somewhat weak and too small to flower in their first year, I had found a way of reproducing the plant. However, it is just as risky as the division of the crown previously described, and should therefore be used only as a last resort.

over it. The moisture-laden atmosphere inside the jar encourages root growth.

If the parent plant is not to be used for breeding purposes, one can wait until flowering has finished. Then one simply cuts the scape a few centimetres above and below the shoot and pushes the cutting into a mixture of sand and peat. In this way the shoot will have a food supply until such time as it can fend for itself. When the remains of the stem begin to rot they should be removed; the plantlet is now ready for planting out in the garden.

The Lanoline-BAP-IAA Method

Years ago when this method had not yet been developed I had the following experience: on the single fan of 'By Myself', which I possessed at that time, crown rot began to set

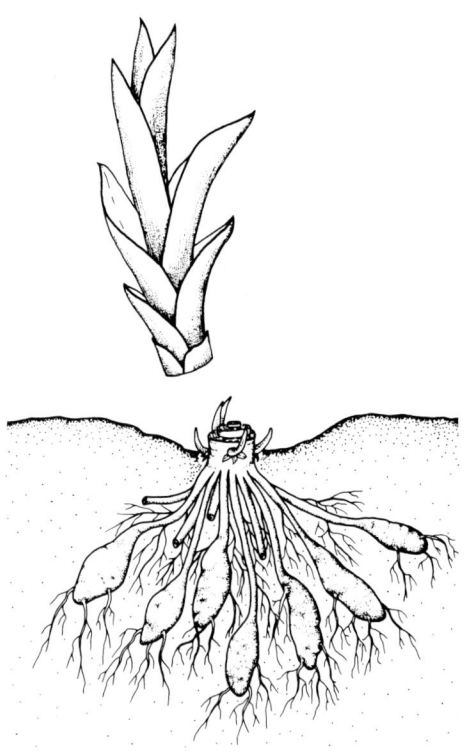

Figure 36 A few weeks after the crown has been cut and treated, new shoots will be observed sprouting from it.

Two American botanists, M. Kasha and J.S. Kirby-Smith, also noticed that day lilies produced new shoots when the top of the crown was cut off, but they took the process a step further by using organic solutions to stimulate such growth. In order to protect the wound from water and prevent incursions by bacteria, the chemicals are prepared in the anhydrous medium, lanoline. The proportions are as follows: 3.0g lanoline to 90mg BAP (6-benzylaminopurine) and 90mg IAA (indole acetic acid). One can also add 160mg DMSO (dimethylsulfoxide) if available, though its absence is not of great significance so far as the experiment is concerned. The ready-mixed solution can be obtained through the American Hemerocallis Society.

Before dealing with the actual procedure, let us first consider whether it is all really worthwhile. The developers of the method claim that one can obtain up to six new shoots in three to four weeks and, with repeated applications, as many as 20 shoots. This method has been in use in the US since about 1981, and increasing numbers of growers there seem to be adopting it. This still begs the question of whether it is worthwhile. Much depends on whether one merely goes in for exchanges, in which case one's friends are surely able to wait just one more year, or whether one is a commercial plant breeder anxious to get produce marketed at the earliest opportunity. In this case the method would seem to be ideal, since neither the amount of work involved nor the expense is too great.

Perhaps some people have already been put off by the technical terminology, but there is really no need to worry. This method is child's play. It is not advisable to dig up the plant and pot it before treatment (this was in fact recommended in the original article in America). Unfortunately, my results were disappointing.

The first step is to scrape away the soil from a well-established plant so that the crown and upper roots are exposed; then cut off the leaf fan at the point where it emerges from the crown. The cut is best made with a single-edged razor blade or a scalpel. It is important that the cut is not made too high, for then the plant will simply keep growing from the original point. The correct time for the operation is the spring, when the plant's new growth is about 5–10cm long. All that then remains is to spread the paste thinly on the cut section. The paste should not be too cold, since it is then not so easy to spread.

When I first tried this method, I used to leave the trench open, which had the advantage that I could repeat the treatment if a heavy shower had washed away the lanoline. Later, however, I noticed that it did not really matter if the hole was refilled. The original instructions recommended removing the new shoots and repeating the treatment, if and when possible, so as to encourage the growth of yet more plantlets. I considered the root systems of these to be rather weak; so I decided to cut up the crown in such a way that each new plant had a few of the old roots. I thought that this would be advisable, since the duration of the experiment was not, as suggested, some four weeks, but much longer, namely more like ten weeks. It seemed best to try to get the cuttings established as quickly as possible, so that they might cope well with the winter, and this is exactly what happened.

It is difficult to assess whether the experiment was an unqualified success. 'Norton Orange' yielded just one extra plantlet, but there were five with 'Ruffled Apricot' and ten with 'Elizabeth Yancey'. Friends in Belgium and south-west Germany who conducted similar trials over the same period also had inconclusive results. Sometimes the treatment even led to total loss. It may be that the greater success rate in America is due to a more favourable climate. Hence the method may be just the thing for the gardener with access to a greenhouse.

Tissue Culture

If someone does succeed in producing a sky-blue day lily, there can be no doubt that it will be in great demand. Consequently it would be very much in the grower's interest to produce as many plants of this kind in the shortest possible time. The previously mentioned methods are fine for everyday purposes, but when it comes to a potential million-dollar earner, such as a possible sky-blue *Hemerocallis*, a professional method is called for. This is where tissue culture comes into its own, though it is more the domain of specialist laboratories than the nurseryman.

The necessary work can be undertaken in a 'kitchen laboratory', provided that conditions are sufficiently sterile and one keeps to the basic rules. Tissue culture involves taking tiny pieces of a plant and turning them into plantlets. Such tiny pieces of the plant are unable to grow on their own; they have to be sustained with nutrients from an external source. The process demands that the plants be raised in sterile conditions, without contamination through fungi or bacteria, in a germ-free medium within a closed, transparent container.

In day lilies the most suitable material for replication is tissue from the flower. M.M. Meyer stated that he took pieces of the flower pedicel 1–2mm thick, or alternatively he cut buds of up to a maximum of 2cm long into six pieces. In the course of his trials he discovered that some stalks are capable of reproduction only in the part immediately adjoining the flower bud. The tissue has to be sterilised by steeping it for 20 minutes in a solution of 0.5 per cent sodium hypochloride and 0.1 per cent polyoxyethylene-sorbitan.

A modified Murashige-Skoog medium, containing 0.1mg/litre naphthalene acetic acid (NAA) and 0.1mg/litre kinetin, will give good reproduction both with stalk sections and bud sections. Compared with the standard medium, the sugar content here has been doubled. A thin stalk section with reversed polarity (i.e. upper side downwards) or a piece of the flower, if placed in this medium and kept in the dark at a temperature of 26°C, produces a callus of about 2cm diameter within four to eight weeks.

The callus portions often display considerable root activity and even in the dark some of them start to form tiny shoots. The majority of the plantlets, however, develop after exposure to light. Later the callus tissue is cut into several pieces and put into the light in a slightly changed medium. The pieces should not be less than 0.5cm across. Under the influence of light new plants develop in a matter of some four to eight weeks. In practice not every piece of callus will turn into a plant, but this method will work at least in part on all types of day lily.

The plantlets that develop should possess evident leaf and root systems and with a little care they may be transplanted into a suitable potting compost (a light mixture of two parts sand, one part loam, one part peat and one part perlite). The plants are fed with a weak fertiliser solution and placed in a shaded spot to harden off. After about ten days the plants are transferred to an ordinary greenhouse and then, when the roots begin to show at the surface of the pot-ball, they can finally be planted out in the garden.

Compared with the Lanoline-BAP-IAA method, the number of plants that can be reproduced through this method is increased not just by a factor of ten, but rather a hundred or even a thousandfold. Even though this method is more expensive than more traditional ones, it clearly justifies the extra cost, if it enables a grower to market a new and improved hybrid very rapidly after many years of preparatory work in developing the strain.

CULTIVATION OF DAY LILIES

Obtaining Plants

Between ten and 20 years ago anyone wishing to obtain a new variety of day lily would have had to import it themselves. Not because the plants were not known, but because the choice was limited to a few old-fashioned, tried and trusted varieties. Over the years matters have gradually improved and more of the newer and more exciting varieties are now available through nurseries, some of which are specialising in *Hemerocallis*. Basically there are two ways to build up a collection of day lilies: firstly, by buying from breeders or nurserymen, and secondly, by exchanging plants with other growers.

As for buying day lilies, it is best to find nurseries that specialise in day lilies (see appendix), for they will have the most recent varieties. A visit to a large garden centre might very well prove fruitless if one is looking for something out of the ordinary; they do cater for the mass market and would probably not be in a position to order one or two plants specially. Some of the mail order catalogues have day lilies on their lists, but sadly these are either only the very old types or the choice is very limited.

The USA is undoubtedly the prime source of new and exotic day lilies and there are US mail order firms who will ship to the UK (see appendix). In some cases the suppliers are also breeders and growers. Mailing costs can be considerable, as can customs dues.

Species from the Far East are best obtained as seeds; some Australian nurseries will export to Britain and Europe.

Planting

If someone presents you with a large clump of one of the older sorts of day lily, then all that is necessary is to plant it in the garden. On the other hand, if one has bought a single fan of a new hybrid at great expense and this has spent quite a while in the mail, then obviously its planting has to be undertaken with very much more care. The first question one needs to consider is whether it is better to order new plants for the spring or for the autumn.

It makes little difference, except that evergreen or semi-evergreen sorts are best planted in the spring. This enables them to develop a sound root system by the autumn. On the other hand, I have also received older dormant types in November and planted them straight away, just bedding them in, and they took no harm. I have even known clumps to be set aside in a corner for the winter and survive without damage. It seems that, during the winter rest period, day lilies are not all that sensitive.

Despite the benefit of air freight, it can sometimes happen that when a day lily arrives it seems to be rather dehydrated. Many books recommend that, if this is the case, the plant should be placed in a weak fertiliser solution overnight. For a long time now I have not bothered with this and have not suffered any losses as a result. Normally a freshly dug-out *Hemerocallis* plant will keep for up to two weeks. Nevertheless it is always as well to replant as soon after the plant's arrival as possible. If, for some reason, there is not the time to do this properly, the plant should be heeled into some moist sand somewhere shady. Then, when the day lily is taken out a few days later, tiny root fibres should already have formed.

In the foregoing I have, of course, assumed that one is dealing with a ready-to-plant *Hemerocallis*. Should this not be the case because, for example, the plant in question is being resited within one's own garden, then it has first to be prepared as follows: trim the leaves

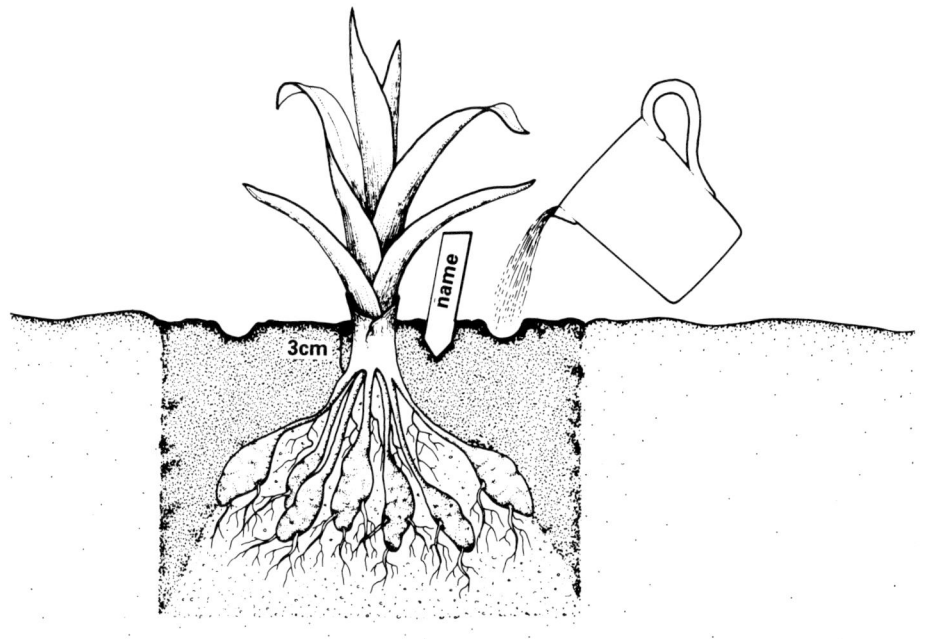

Figure 37 When planting, spread the roots around the heap of soil in the bottom of the hole.

into a fan shape, the length to be commensurate with the height of the plant, and if the roots are long these too can be shortened to about 15–20cm. Both these measures help to promote a more rapid settling in of the day lily. Care should be taken not to include any rotten or damaged pieces of root.

If the soil where the day lilies are to be planted consists of newly-cleared ground, it should be dug over to a depth of 30cm. It is also advisable to work in some compost or well-rotted manure and peat. If the ground has been cultivated previously, simply dig a hole that is slightly wider than the root ball. Next a small mound of soil is built up in the bottom of the hole and the plant is set on this with the roots hanging down the sides of the mound, evenly spread out. Then the hole can be filled again using either the soil originally dug out, or a mixture of soil, compost, peat, sand and well-rotted manure.

New plants should be planted to the same depth as that at which they were growing originally. The leaves will be blanched where they were below ground, but green above. For evergreen plants obtained from the south of the USA, it is probably a good idea to bury the crown a little deeper than this mark, in order to provide greater frost protection. Usually the plant is set 3–5cm below the surface of the soil, but on no account should it be deeper than 10cm. When refilling the hole, the soil should be well worked in between the roots, so as to avoid pockets of air where the roots could dry out. The best way is to water in the roots and when that water has soaked into the ground, fill in the hole and draw a small irrigation trench around the plant.

Regardless of whether the newly-planted variety is slow or quick-growing it should have enough room to develop. Whereas the new miniature varieties need only 30–40cm between plants, the large tetraploids need to be at least 40–60cm apart. It is not just that tightly packed *Hemerocallis* plants will hinder each other's growth, or indeed grow into one another, but rather that such crowding detracts from the overall effect. (See also the section 'Making The Most of Day Lilies'.) If, as well as building up a collection of day lilies, one wants to exchange specimens, then correct labelling is important and should be done immediately upon planting. So long as it is only a matter of up to ten plants and each of these of a different colour, one might be able to rely on memory, but plants lose value if they cannot be identified.

Siting

So far we have dealt with the actual planting, but not the siting. There are several points to watch. Broadly speaking, day lilies will flourish in all types of soil and in any kind of situation, though clearly with varying degrees of success. Thus *Hemerocallis* is good for bordering ponds or lakes, but does not tolerate actually standing in water. Even though the plants like a nice fresh soil, they abhor stagnant conditions. This is something to watch out for when one is planting alongside a stream. In general it is advisable when planting out a water garden, that is to say along its margin, to keep to the older, well-proven types of day lily.

If soil conditions are problematic, raised beds might be advisable: good permeable garden soil should be heaped to a height of 15–20cm within some kind of edging. Planted in this way the *Hemerocallis* plants are not likely to suffer from too moist a soil. However, in order to guard against drying out, regular watering is necessary.

There are really no special rules to observe so far as the composition of the soil is concerned. One should, of course, go by the old axiom for improving the ground: if the soil is heavy, add sand and humus and if the soil is sandy, add compost and peat. Naturally the type of soil dictates how it should be fed. There is no point in adding slow-acting fertilisers to porous, sandy soil, for these will be leached out into the subsoil long before they can take effect.

When choosing somewhere for a new plant, one has to consider whether the site is shady or sunny. Both possibilities are viable, but the sunnier the site the more flowers there will be. Day lilies will, in fact, grow where other plants might fail, but without the sun much of their effect is lost. Above all, light yellow, pink and pastel colours require a great deal of light to enhance their delicate colours. Things are slightly different for darker colours, the purples and dark reds; these colours absorb heat and light, and so the flowers could well shrivel up in the midday sun of high summer. Choose instead somewhere half-shady for these, especially in hot climates.

Unfortunately a position in partial shade also has a disadvantage: the flower scapes tend to bend towards the light and become etiolated. But there is an advantage for the plant breeder, because plants in such sites tend to produce more seeds; possibly fertilisation suffers in too much heat. There seems to be some difference of opinion about these things, which may be due to geographical factors.

Finally we should consider the cultivation of day lilies in tubs, pots and containers. Small-growing sorts such as 'Stella d'Oro' and 'Happy Returns' are ideal for tub culture on a patio and give many months of flower. The larger sorts are generally less satisfactory in tubs. If grown in tubs they need to be positioned in full sun. They should be planted in a good free-draining compost, and fed and watered every week throughout the growing season.

Watering and Mulching

Although day lilies do not like to be swamped, they still need plenty of water, because, like other plants, they consist of at least 90 per cent water. Most of this water is in the cells, but water is also the medium that carries the nutrients on which the plants depend.

In a normal British summer where a few days' sunshine are often followed by several rainy ones, day lilies need no extra watering, though during long dry spells they suffer as much as other plants.

Water is very important during the spring, when the scapes and buds are being formed, and the summer, during the flowering period. For reblooming varieties watering plays a very special part; apparently a sufficient moisture content of the soil is one of the factors that determines whether or not the plant produces a second crop of flowers. A most important aspect of watering is in connection with feeding, and one should always pay strict attention to the instructions that accompany the fertiliser being used. It is all too easy to damage plants by misusing fertilisers.

As long as the ground feels cool and moist to the touch it is wet enough and there is no need to buy a special moisture meter. If, however, the ground feels warm and dry, or even a little dusty, then it is time to water. A gentle daily sprinkling is not nearly as effective as the occasional soaking, which allows the water to penetrate deeper into the ground. Surface dampness tends simply to evaporate again. A daily soaking is not necessary for day lilies, because the roots are able to act as storage organs.

Spraying with a hose can have unforeseen consequences. It goes without saying that this should never be done in the middle of the day when it is hot. But even if it is carried out in the evening, sprinkling *Hemerocallis* with water can have an adverse effect, especially if they are in bud. When the flowers open on the following day they may well be marked, particularly those of darker colours. If one is anxious to have the garden looking at its best for some special occasion, it is best to avoid watering the day before. If one does, use the kind of perforated hose that will water the ground but not the plant.

One should, of course, be careful not to overwater the plants. Day lilies are very adept at taking up water and are able to store it in their thick fleshy roots. Overwatering can also easily wash away valuable nutrients.

The need to water can be greatly reduced if the bed has been well mulched. Mulching is the laying of a blanket, usually of organic matter, over the soil to conserve moisture, help activate the soil and suppress weeds. The mulch material should be easy to apply, have a long duration and a good appearance, retain moisture, be inexpensive and easily obtainable.

Forest bark incorporates all the necessary features. It provides a long-lasting mulch that is easy to apply and does not have to be too thick; it conserves moisture well and is readily available. Spent mushroom compost is also an excellent mulch. There is a kind of chaff-cutter or garden-shredder with which garden waste can be turned into mulch material. One needs to be careful though: branches with thorns can be painful when one handles the mulch later, because the thorns never seem to rot down as quickly as the rest. Even wood will rot down bit by bit and in the process take up nitrogen. For this reason the latter needs to be put back into the soil. A slow-acting fertiliser is best and this should be applied before the mulch layer is put down.

It is also possible to use leaf mould or pine needles, though these have disadvantages as well. Pine needles are not that easy to obtain and need to be applied thickly if they are to keep down weeds. Leaves, especially oak leaves, eventually turn into an excellent humus, but initially they tend to blow about in windy weather and to collect just where one does not want them. It is a much better idea to collect them in heaps and to allow them to turn into leaf mould first. In fact, any compost, whether fully composted or only partly composted, provides a good mulch.

The day lilies themselves can play their parts in this recycling process. Each autumn I tend to trim off all my plants, even the evergreens, to just above ground level. The evergreens will very soon begin to sprout again, but I have never found that any harm ensued. The leaves are then chopped up in a shredder. If this is to be used mainly for *Hemerocallis* leaves, the type that has a cylinder cutter is better than a star-shaped cutter blade, for which the leaves are really too soft and bendy. Also the leaves should be shredded before they have turned yellow, for then they become leathery. This means that the leaves should be cut back while there is still some sap in them.

Fertilisers and General Care

Day lilies do best in neutral to mildly acid soils, though they will grow perfectly well in alkaline soils and with a little encouragement even on chalk. Very poor or sandy soils that tend to leach out easily should be treated with a compound fertiliser several times during the spring and early summer ($N:P:K = 5:10:5$ or $5:10:10$). For the average garden, however, one good application of fertiliser in the early spring should suffice. Over-application will not ensure more flowers, but simply lusher plants with more foliage.

The fertiliser should be applied as instructed on the packet and care must be taken to keep it from the leaves of the day lilies so as to prevent damage. It is also advisable to water the ground after spreading the fertiliser, unless rain is expected. As a rule newly-planted day lilies should not be given fertiliser until they have become established. For these mulching with compost is preferable. Older and larger clumps of day lilies require more feeding than younger ones, not only because the soil will have become depleted of nutrients, but also because the plant itself may need revitalising.

Many *Hemerocallis* growers apply fertiliser again during the early autumn, but such soil improvement needs to have been completed before the day lilies start their winter rest period, or it will be ineffective. Another point is that a late summer or early autumn fertiliser should not contain so much nitrogen ($N:P:K = 3:12:12$ or $4:8:12$), because nitrogen encourages renewed growth and this is not desirable at this stage of the year. On the other hand, phosphorus and potassium (K) stimulate the formation of flower buds for the coming year.

Even so, all day lilies that are to be mulched should be given fertiliser once more before the mulch is applied. This is because, as the mulching material decays, it absorbs nitrogen from the soil and so creates a short-term nitrogen deficiency. The nitrogen, which the organic matter needs for the process of decay, is best fed to it directly as fertiliser and this works best if it is on the soil under, rather than on top of, the mulch layer.

It does not matter all that much which compound fertiliser is used, though it should be remembered that for day lilies it is mainly the phosphorus and potassium content that counts. Nitrogen needs to be present in the soil only in sufficient proportion to provide adequate plant growth. Too much nitrogen produces yellowish foliage in the early spring, becoming a luxuriant and sappy green only later in the season. An excess of fertiliser is particularly damaging for red and purple varieties, being responsible for their flowers becoming flabby and wilting in the heat of summer. Moreover there is a tendency toward fewer but longer flower stalks and poorer blooms. Not least, a surplus of nitrogen can have an adverse effect on the winter-hardiness of the plant.

As well as getting the feeding right, another question that is frequently asked is about weeding. This is usually only a problem with younger plants, since older ones with their abundant foliage suppress weeds that have seeded themselves. On the whole I do not favour the use of chemicals in the garden, but sometimes the weed infestation is such that this is the only way to beat the problem. If this step becomes necessary, then take advice on the kind of weedkiller to use, and, above all, heed the manufacturer's instructions. I much prefer mulching or hoeing and weeding by hand. When loosening the soil one needs to work fairly shallowly, so as to avoid the tiny absorbant roots of the *Hemerocallis* plants, which lie close to the surface.

The appearance of a garden can be enhanced if even those day lilies that have finished blooming look reasonably neat and tidy. To what extent and how often one actually inspects one's garden, dead-heading where the blooms have not fallen off by themselves, is a personal affair. It is not something that has to be done on a regular basis. In fact, if one intends gathering the seeds, it should not be done at all so far as the designated capsules are concerned. However, those flowers on the plant that have not been specifically pollinated should be removed to encourage those that have.

In certain unfavourable weather conditions it is probably sensible to remove the fallen flowers from the ground around the plant. This is to prevent mould setting in during prolonged periods of wet weather; such mould could spread to the plant itself. Throughout the entire growing period any damaged or diseased foliage needs to be removed so that the plant as a whole will not suffer.

Diseases and Pests

Not for nothing are day lilies called 'flowers for the intelligent idler'. They need but little attention and suffer few diseases or pests. The only problem apart from leaf spot, which has occurred in my garden during the last few years, has been crown rot. As for pests, apart from slugs, snails and hemerocallis flies, my garden seems remarkably free of them, despite the very great number of plants.

There are two kinds of **crown rot**:

bacterial soft rot and a granular fungal rot. Although the causes are not the same, the effects are similar. Leaves that have recently sprouted stop growing, turn yellow and finally go mushy. If one takes hold of them in this state, one can easily pull them out. The seat of the trouble is clearly in the crown and once this has rotted the plant is dead. Crown rot occurs mainly in the spring and is not that difficult to control.

Bacterial soft rot results from damage to the roots or crown so that bacteria, such as *rhizoctonia*, can penetrate the plant tissue, but a second type of rot is caused by a fungus, *Cercosphora hemerocallis*, which is similar to ergot. With soft rot the intruding bacteria turn healthy plant tissue into a smelly pulp. Moist conditions, when the soil has compacted round the roots so as to exclude air, favour rapid multiplication of the bacteria. This kind of rot attacks newly-planted or freshly-separated plants. Fungal crown rot is not particularly common in Europe. The effect is a layer of tiny, brownish-blackish spore sacs looking rather like mustard seeds. The fungus produces a white, thread-like network of fibre, reminiscent of cotton wool, which quickly spreads over the crown and among the leaves.

Although the actual treatment for crown rot is relatively easy to carry out, it has to be stressed that the success rate is only about 50 per cent. Nevertheless it is always worth having a go. As soon as one finds that there is something wrong with a particular day lily, it should be dug out, at the latest when mushy leaves become evident. Then with a clean knife, or scalpel, cut away any tissue which is rotten until only those parts of the crown which are firm and white are left. The crown should then be dusted with a fungicide and replanted in a new place. If the plant recovers, a new rank of leaves will grow, and sometimes even several. The effect of the treatment is therefore akin to the Lanoline-BAP-IAA method.

Although much has been written about **spring sickness**, it does not seem to be an actual disease. It attacks only the tender inner leaves of a given fan. The leaves turn brown and rot down to the ground. The tips of the scapes are not themselves damaged, but generally cannot manage to push their way through the mushy matter of the rotted leaves. Consequently the plant ceases to grow. It can be assumed that symptoms of this nature can occur in specific climatic regions where alternating periods of frost and thaw or late frost can damage day lilies. All rotten tissue needs to be removed, even if it means having to dig out the plants in the process. However, no chemicals are necessary for the treatment.

Leaf spots are phenomena that occur quite frequently, especially on the newer super-varieties. Not for nothing were the historical varieties listed in the 'Making the Choice' chapter, for among them this disease is a rare occurrence. Perhaps in their quest for ever newer and more exotic flowers, breeders have lost sight of the plants as a whole. Whether or not one takes steps to treat leaf spots depends on their overall effect on the look of the plants. The damage is caused by types of *botrytis* or *colle-*

totrichum. These do not actually harm *Hemerocallis*, which is not the case with lilies. Leaves that have turned completely yellow have to be removed and as a preventive measure sprayed with a fungicide effective against downy mildew.

The only pest that can definitely be harmful to day lilies is the **hemerocallis gall fly** (*Contarinia quinquenotata*). This tiny insect uses its ovipositor to place its eggs into the newly-formed buds of *Hemerocallis* plants. As the larvae develop they devour the bud from the inside. The result is that instead of becoming longer the bud merely becomes wider in the course of time, misshapen and often split down the side. If one opens the bud one finds tiny white maggots inside. The only effective treatment is with chemical sprays that are highly toxic and really too dangerous to use in the garden.

My own method of waging war on the hemerocallis gall fly is simplicity itself. I keep a sharp eye on the buds during early summer, looking for damage of the kind described above. It seems that the insect has distinct preferences, one of which is an early variety called 'Limited Edition'. Any bud that shows signs of attack is removed (it is really only a very small percentage) and dropped into a plastic bag. When I have completed the inspection I seal the bag and drop it into the dustbin. The fewer gall flies that survive, the less damage will be done the following year.

Aphids do not appear to be a problem so far as day lilies are concerned. I once found that my *Iris sibirica* was thickly covered in black fly, yet they scorned a *Hemerocallis*

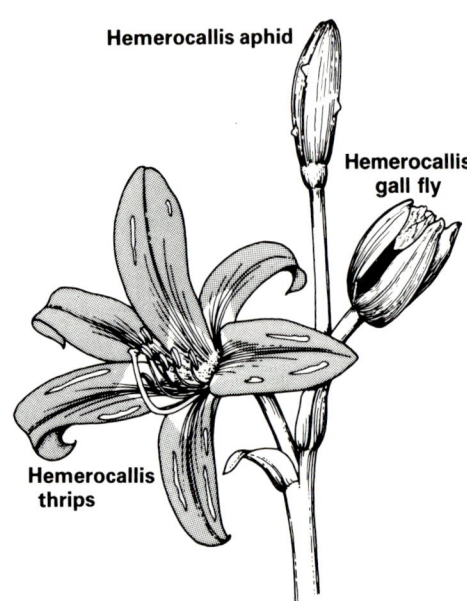

Figure 38 The type of damage caused by the three main *Hemerocallis* pests.

growing alongside. There is, however, an aphid that is specific to *Hemerocallis*, called the **hemerocallis fly** (*Myzus hemerocallis*). This has so far not reached the UK, but it is presumably only a matter of time. There are a number of sure signs that indicate attack by this creature: one is the absence of light green colouring in very young leaves, and another is white spots on the foliage. A closer examination of these show them to be scales of skin from the insects. Another thing that will be noticed is the honey-dew that these insects exude. The leaves become sticky and attract ants.

This particular kind of aphid can also cause damage to buds. The insect feeds on the sap from the buds and causes wart-like protrusions on them as well as malformed flowers.

'Frank Gladney' (Durio, 1979 USA)

'Mini Skirt' (Lambert, 1966 USA)

'Sari' (Munson, 1983 USA)

'Cleo Barnwell' (Stutson, 1972 USA)

'Lullaby Baby' (Spalding, 1975 USA)

'Fairy Tale Pink' (Pierce, 1980 USA)

Pink *Hemerocallis* varieties

'Jade Star' (Moldovan, 1978 USA)

'Chicago Nobby' (Marsh, 1974 USA)

'Catherine Woodberry' (Childs, 1967 USA)

'Forget Me Not' (Brown-Lankart, 1971 USA)

'Shinto Shrine' (Moldovan, 1975 USA)

'Serene Madonna' (Childs, 1972 USA)

Blue and white *Hemerocallis* varieties

'Berlin Premiere' (Tamberg, 1979 FRG)

'Berlin Eyed' (Tamberg, FRG not registered)

'Cologne Morning Glow' (Stobberg, FRG not registered)

'Vienna Butterfly' (Zelina, Austria, not registered)

'Pfennigparade' (Köhlein, 1981, FRG)

Hemerocallis hybrids from central Europe

Hemerocallis selection. In the grounds of the Palm Garden in Frankfurt day lilies have been planted extensively. There is also a special section for central European and miniature varieties. The two detail pictures show examples of miniature varieties.

'Siloam Bo Peep' (Henry, 1978 USA)

'Little Women' (Wild, 1969 USA)

Those blooms that do open tend to suffer from colour aberrations. These aphids multiply with great rapidity while the temperature is not too high, in early spring and in the autumn. Any of the proprietary brands for spraying against sap-feeding insects, green or black fly, are effective.

It is amazing how many creatures have adapted themselves to specific plants: there is also a specific **hemerocallis thrips** (*Frankliniella hemerocallis*). This grey-black pest is about the same size as the upper part of an exclamation mark (!). Once the flowers have opened, the thrips can cause no further damage. What this insect does is to prise its way into a bud that is just about to open; in the process it forces its body against the still tightly-packed petals, rupturing the cells and causing bleeding, thereby providing itself with the desired meal. When the flower does eventually open, there will be white marks on the segments, which show up particularly clearly on the darker colours. Occasionally the bleeding causes the segments to adhere to each other so that the flower can no longer open properly. If the infestation is severe, a whole plant can be crippled. However, the pest is not all that common and is one with which it is possible to live.

Nematodes constitute no special problem as far as day lilies are concerned. They attack only those plants that have already been weakened in some way, or whose roots have been damaged. There are many kinds of these tiny threadworms. Some devour the vital root hairs and so deprive the day lily of its ability to absorb moisture. Others eat their way into the roots, causing rot or disruption of the vascular tissue. Some produce toxins after penetration and so cause damage to the plant.

However, this is not so much a specific *Hemerocallis* problem as one concerning the soil. If one has a nematode problem it is best to seek advice. One of the questions one is bound to be asked is whether potatoes are being grown nearby, since there seems to be a link between potatoes and nematodes. Clearly when day lilies are cultivated for commercial purposes one must be able to give an assurance that the plants are nematode-free; as a primary precaution day lilies and potatoes should never be grown in close proximity. As a preventive measure importation of plants into the UK requires a special certificate and HM Customs keep a watch at ports of entry.

Slugs and **snails** can also be a real problem. A serious infestation can result from giving day lilies a winter mulch and failing to remove it again early enough in the spring. Shielded from direct sunlight slugs and snails find the moist soil conditions an ideal habitat and the fresh day lily shoots very much to their liking; indeed they manage to consume these much faster than they are able to regrow. The best ways to combat slugs and snails are by paying proper attention to garden hygiene and using slug pellets as necessary.

MAKING THE MOST OF DAY LILIES

In the Garden

Few perennials lend themselves quite so well to garden landscaping as do day lilies. Not only are they adaptable to a wide range of conditions, they also come in a great variety of sizes, colours and colour combinations. This makes it very easy to use them in exciting ways. Simplicity produces the greatest impact and the overall scheme needs planning, care and above all taste. Preference for a particular flower and its use for hybridising need not be an obstacle.

In laying out a garden, just as in any other art form, one should always keep the overall impression in mind rather than concentrating on individual elements. Thus *Hemerocallis*, like any other plants one is using, are not in themselves of prime importance but should be considered as constituents of the whole. One should avoid a general hotchpotch, with plants stuck here and there with no particular order. Whether one is starting a garden from scratch, or incorporating day lilies in an existing garden, one needs first to consider the following points:

Are day lilies to be the dominant feature or merely a lesser decorative element?

Does the background demand tall, medium or low-growing day lilies, or a mixture of various heights?

Is the planting to have a peak period of blooming, or is it to be colourful throughout the year?

What sizes or colours of day lilies will go with, or set off existing plants?

Is the intention to have fragrant, night-flowering varieties near a terrace where they could be lit up at night?

Are there areas of partial shade where dark-flowered varieties could thrive?

There is now such a wide choice of day lilies available that it is possible to find varieties that will suit just about every situation and purpose. On the whole it is best to plan one's effects, rather than try to make up a garden from an odd assortment of plants bought on the spur of the moment in a garden centre. Prime consideration should be given as to whether a particular variety is right for its particular place in the garden and the other plants among which it is to grow. Giant-flowering or patterned varieties, for example, pose special problems. The latter are more effective against quiet backgrounds; an excess of colour can be very restless.

Day lilies are eminently suitable for landscaping in public places, such as pedestrian precincts, outside hotels, offices, hospitals and so forth, as well as parks. Their usefulness in garden or general landscaping has so far not been fully exploited in Britain and Europe. One needs, however, to distinguish between landscaping and show varieties. The latter may well have the more exotic blooms, but landscaping demands something lasting, with plenty of flowers in harmonious colours; here even plants with minor flower defects can be of use if the foliage is healthy and fresh-looking.

Foliage is especially important where day lilies are to be used as ground cover: on slopes, along fences, paths and boundaries, as well as around memorials, statues and buildings. Since the rich foliage will virtually arrest the seeding and growth of weeds, it is simply a matter of ensuring that the plants are planted close enough at the outset. The landscape gardener will therefore seek out the older and well-proven sorts that are not too costly. With older varieties one does not have to wait for ages for a small fan of leaves to become a well-established plant, as is so often the case with the newer ones.

Attention should also be paid to the material of which a house is constructed, as well as other garden features. Light yellow day lilies show up best in front of dark wood, red bricks or tiles, for example. If the house happens to have a white or other light-coloured finish, then the darker types of *Hemerocallis* come into their own. Modern ruffled or patterned varieties need to be planted where they catch the eye and can be fully appreciated.

What happens, though, if one starts collecting day lilies with much the same dedication as, say, a stamp collector shows towards his stamps? Sometimes one comes across a garden in which day lilies have been planted in rows, as if they were vegetables on an allotment, or as they might be in a nursery garden – not very effective, in my opinion. If the garden is big enough, muster the plants in beds. Even more effective is a garden on several levels with *Hemerocallis* bordering the paths. A collection of a large number of different varieties can make an exciting and powerful impact, but only if the plants have been set out with care. There are several possibilities:

> In mixed planting one needs to pay careful attention to adjacent colours; a bluish-pink and melon clash, for example.
>
> It is best to plant a group of one colour to contrast with a similarly-sized group of another colour, e.g. deep red contrasting with cream or pale yellow.
>
> Set out the day lilies in beds with each devoted to a different

colour, e.g. a bed for red varieties, another for yellows and so on.

Stagger the colours one behind the other from the lightest to the darkest, say cream-pink-red.

On the whole it does not really matter which approach one takes, be it a colourful mixture or contrasting colours, a uniform mass or graded colours. Each is effective and equally good. It is planting undertaken with no particular purpose in mind that does not look good. The purpose can also be lost if, in the course of time, an older specimen is taken out here and there and replaced by a newer hybrid that does not fit in with the scheme. I tend not to rely merely on descriptions of new acquisitions, but always plant them out on their own in a separate bed so that I may see for myself. Here they can develop in peace and be sorted out before being added to the main collection. Day lilies need not be confined to beds of herbaceous perenninals. *Hemerocallis* of the older sorts, such as 'Corky', 'Bitsy', 'Lemon Bells' and 'Golden Chimes', also lend themselves remarkably well to settings among foliage trees, evergreens and roses. The lavenders and purples with green throats are particularly effective grown with roses, especially the smaller sorts like 'Little Grapette' and 'Water Witch'.

Another very pretty way of using day lilies is to place a single specially selected day lily some distance in front of a conifer. For instance, one could combine one of the older types of day lily called 'Anzak', which is a beautiful red, with the silver fir (*Abies procera* 'Glauca'), which has silvery-blue needles. In my garden I have a number of day lilies growing under various kinds of maple. One must ensure that the trees growing in close proximity to the day lilies have loose crowns, allowing light to filter through. Ideally the *Hemerocallis* should be planted on the sunny side because in shade they do not flower so freely.

Day lilies are also well suited to planting at the water's edge, although, as has already been said, the plants themselves do not like to grow in wet ground. Indeed, massed plantings of the reliable old yellow day lilies, or melons or pinks, are especially effective beside water, and their large green clumps of foliage make a good edging for this sort of garden feature. Artificial ponds create no problem since the banks of these are normally quite dry, but with natural lakes or ponds one would need to avoid swampy areas and in any case try out those older and well-proven sorts that can withstand a very moist soil. The modern Californian types are quite unsuitable for this sort of setting.

If you prefer something fragrant in the garden, there are several day lilies with this attribute. They need to be planted in a sunny situation that is shielded from the wind so that their fragrance can hang on the air. Ideally the site should be close to a part of the garden where people sit, such as a terrace or patio, or bordering one of the main paths, so as to make the most of the fragrance.

It is worth considering *Hemerocallis* species for this purpose for it is among these that the purest and strongest fragrances are to be found. *H. altissima* together with a shrub rose, for example, is a combination that is not easily bettered either visually or for its scent. The species are also particularly suited for other special purposes. Because *H. lilio-asphodelus* will tolerate wet ground, it can be grown in conjunction with other moisture-loving plants such as *Iris sibirica*, but also look wonderful in a conventional border with *Iris* 'Gerald Darby'. On the other hand, *H. dumortieri* and *H. middendorffii*, like bearded irises, are ideal for hot, dry situations. If small day lilies are needed, then *H. minor* fits the bill, but the diminutive 'Eenie' hybrids might be too strident for a rock garden. On the whole, the species are probably too often passed over by day lily growers in favour of more modern hybrids.

Companion Plants

Day lilies are extraordinarily versatile plants, which is why they fit so easily into almost any garden setting. And if they are to be the dominant plant in the garden, there is a whole host of other plants that can be used to show them off to best effect. Yellow day lilies are most effective among light blue and red plants; the red varieties are best in a setting of dark blue, yellow and cream (white contrasts too harshly); purple and blue tones are enhanced by light and pink hues, while pink-coloured day lilies look best against silvers and greys.

The actual choice of companion plants will depend not only on colour, but also on dimension and flowering times. However, since colour is the main criterion, the list of companion plants is arranged by colour. First, though, I would like to mention one plant in particular, the narcissus. To my mind narcissi are the ideal partners for day lilies, for they bloom earlier and then, when their leaves turn yellow, any unsightliness is concealed by the foliage of the *Hemerocallis*.

Blue, Violet, Lavender

Aconitum × *bicolour* (Monkshood), bright to dark blue VI–VII,* 100–150cm.
   'Bressingham Spire', deep violet, VII–VIII, 90cm.
Agapanthus Headborne Hybrids and in variety (African Lily), large heads of starry-blue, VI–X, from 20cm to 100cm.
Aster novi-belgii 'Climax', healthy Spode-blue, IX–X, 150cm.
Aster thomsonii 'Nanus', lilac-blue, VIII–IX, 20cm.
Aster × *frikartii* 'Mönch', light blue, VI–IX, 70cm.
Baptisia australis, (False Indigo), dark violet, VI–VII, 100cm.
Campanula glomerata 'Superba', clusters of dark violet, VI–VII, 75cm.
   lactiflora 'Pritchard', violet, VI–VII, 50cm.
   persicifolia, the peach-leaf bell flower, in variety, also white, VII–VIII, 80cm.
Delphinium × *hybridum*, requires firm rooting; VI–VIII, 150–200cm.
Eryngium × *zabellii* 'The Jewel', silvery-blue spikes of blue-mauve, VI–VIII, 90cm.
Geranium grandiflorum, lilac-blue, V–VII, 40cm.
   'Johnson's Blue', cup-shaped bright blue flowers, V–VIII, 30cm.

*Roman numerals denote the months when the plants are in flower.

MAKING THE MOST OF DAY LILIES

wallichianum 'Buxton's Blue', white-eyed blue flowers, V–VIII, 30cm.
Iris 'Gerald Darby', purplish-blue stems, deep blue flowers, V–VI, 70cm.
  sibirica in variety, likes damp, many blues, pinks and whites, VI, 50–100cm.
Lobelia siphilitica, good cutting flower, VIII–X, 80cm.
Penstemon 'Sour Grapes', unusual shade of purplish-green, VI–IX, 90cm.
Salvia haematodes 'Lye End', spikes of deep blue, VI–VIII, 100cm.
  superba, spikes of violet-purple, VII–IX, 100cm.
Tradescantia virginiana, in variety, VI–IX, 45cm.
Veronica teucrium 'Crater Lake Blue', deep blue, VI–VIII, 30cm.
  'Shirley Blue', bright blue, VI–VIII, 20cm.

Yellow, Orange, Red

Achillea 'Gold Plate', flat deep yellow heads, VI–VIII, 60cm.
  'Moonshine', flat pale-yellow heads, VI–VIII, 60cm.
Monarda, Bergamot, in variety, needs moisture, VII–IX, 90cm.
Penstemon, in variety, slightly tender, VII–X, 75cm.
Phlox paniculata, in variety, VIII–IX, 80–100cm.
Polygonum, in variety, VI–IX, 50–90cm.

White

Achillea ptarmica 'The Pearl', double white button flowers in loose heads, VI–VIII, 75cm.

Aruncus dioicus 'Kneiffii' (Goat's Beard), wild flower, creamy-white, VI–VII, 130cm.
Aster divaricatus (Michaelmas Daisy), white, brown centre, IX–X, 60cm.
Astilbe 'Deutschland', needs moisture, VI–VIII, 50cm.
  'Bumalda', needs moisture, VI–VIII, 30cm.
Galtonia candicans, white spikes, VII–VIII, 75cm.
Gaura lindheimeri, long-lasting flower spikes, VII–IX, 80cm.
Monarda, Bergamot, 'Snow Maiden', needs moisture, VIII–IX, 90cm.
Penstemon 'Snow Storm', slightly tender, VII–X, 75cm.
Phlox paniculata, 'White Admiral', 'Miss Lingard', VII–IX, 75cm.
Sanguisorba tenuifolia 'Alba', needs warmth, VIII, 180cm.
Tradescantia virginiana 'Innocence', VI–IX, 40cm.
Yucca flaccida, dark green drooping tipped leaves, white flowers, VIII–X, 120cm.
  filamentosa 'Ivory', pale cream spikes, VIII–X, 120cm.

Ornamental Grasses

Arundo donax 400cm.
Calamagrostis × *acutiflora*, not invasive, 150cm.
Carex montana, always tidy, 20cm.
Carex muskingumensis, graceful, 20–40cm.
Carex pendula, weeping habit, 150cm.
Cortaderia selloana 'Pumila' (Pampas Grass), dwarf type, only 100cm.
Deschampsia cespitosa assorted, 100cm.
Miscanthus sinensis, 'Purpurascens', 'Silver Feather', 200cm.

Molinia caerulea 'Variegata', mottled, 100cm.
Panicum virgatum, sturdy, fragrant, 170cm.
Pennisetum alopecuroides (syn. *P. japonicum*), likes a warm spot, 150cm.
Pennisetum orientale (syn. *P. setaceum*), loose, violet-tinged ears, 60cm.
Sasa tesselata, arched growth, 120cm.
Shibataea kumasaca, not rampant, compact, 60cm.
Sinarundinaria nitida, gigantic, evergreen, 300cm.
Sorghastrum avenaceum, tufty, late-blooming, 120cm.
Stipa barbata, sparsely-leaved tufts, silvery silky and feathery plume, 80cm.
Thamnocalamus spathaceus, do not trim back! 200cm.
Themeda triandra var. *japonica*, protect in winter, 50cm.

Day Lilies in Floral Art

It may seem odd to use in flower arrangements blooms that last for only a day. One often hears people say that *Hemerocallis* are fine for the garden, but are no use for picking. But in fact day lilies can be used in arrangements, as is demonstrated in the USA, where they evaluate not only cut flowers but also arrangements, which may qualify for the 'Mabel Y. Yaste Award'. There is even a prize for the best tricolour arrangement, which is chosen from photographs ('Tricolor Trophy').

Although there is nothing against gathering a simple bouquet of day lilies, they are much more effective if properly displayed. Even a single

Figure 39 Simplicity is the essence of this day lily arrangement.

bloom can be used for this and be replaced each day. The first thing is to find a suitable container into which to set a few branches of berberis, *Euonymus atropurpureus*, or cherry laurel. These keep for a long time and form an attractive background for one or more day lilies, which can be replaced each morning either with a similar bloom or a different colour as required. It takes no more than a moment to remove the old bloom and position a new one in its place with flower wire; in this way

Figure 40 A combination of day lilies and summer flowers makes a beautiful arrangement.

an arrangement can be kept going for a very long time.

To make an arrangement that will last for several days without attention one needs to use a scape with a number of well-developed buds, which will then open in succession over as many days as there are buds. Such an arrangement might also include delphiniums, *Gaillardia*, gladioli, snapdragons, globe thistles, zinnias and *Phlox*. Instead of the narrow day lily leaves, use those of *Canna*, *Hosta*, *Iris* or paeony. Again, structure can be given to the arrangement by the use of a graceful branch or two of berberis, *Cotoneaster*, yew or burning bush. The contrast between yellow day lily flowers and greyish foliage looks attractive.

When building up an arrangement one should bear in mind certain basic structural principles. Strive for a pleasing shape, an interesting silhouette, balance, harmonious colours and good proportions. The container (bowl, vase or whatever) plays a key role: colour and shape should determine the choice. It is important that the arrangement should not become top-heavy, which could easily happen considering the size of some *Hemerocallis* flowers. To avoid this, buds and smaller blooms should be placed near the apex and the larger ones nearer the base. If all the flowers are of similar size, then the darker colours should make up the lower part of the design.

If you have to show your day lily arrangements during late evening, use long-blooming varieties or cut the scapes you intend to use very early in the morning and keep them in a refrigerator until you need to use them.

Photographing Day Lilies

If one is not familiar with plant photography, it is probably best to begin by reading one of the many books on the subject. Just because one may have been taking photographs for years, it does not necessarily follow that the pictures one takes will be good enough to exhibit or publish. Such, at any rate, was my experience when I began serious flower photography.

Picture Format

The first decision is whether to opt for a 35mm camera, giving an image of 24mm × 36mm, or one that uses roll film and gives a larger image,

6cm × 6cm (2¼ × 2¼in). The former is perfectly adequate for producing the occasional picture of publication quality and, in fact, has the advantage of offering a greater depth of focus, especially in the domain of photomacrography,* i.e. close-ups. On the other hand, in garden photography the further away one gets from the subject, the more difficult photography becomes, because the flower heads appear no bigger than pinheads. To some extent this can be offset with a sharper, i.e. a less sensitive, film. However, another difficulty then immediately arises: a film rated 25 ASA is effectively harder than one of 200 ASA,[†] which means that it cannot even out wide differences of contrast. Hence absolutely correct and very even illumination becomes essential.

Since an image of 6cm × 6cm (2¼ × 2¼in) clearly has a much greater surface area than one that measures 24mm × 36mm, the grain size is not of such paramount importance. Obviously the smaller image needs the greater enlargement and the magnification emphasises the grain and thus the lack of sharpness. However, when using the 6cm (2¼in) square format, if one tries to obtain a greater depth of focus by stopping down the lens aperture, yet another limiting factor manifests itself: the resolution of the object lens diminishes proportionally. In practice this means that the image, from the foreground to the background, seems sharp enough, but on examination with a magnifying glass it will be seen to be not as sharp in comparison as the image produced with a medium aperture of between 8 and 11. This effect is brought about by the increased diffusion of light at very small apertures.

Anyone especially interested in close-up photography should aim to be equipped properly from the outset. The worst possible solution is to buy just any auxiliary lens to fit on the front of the camera lens. Better, but not yet best, is the dedicated supplementary lens produced specifically for a particular camera objective. Another, though somewhat impractical, solution for single lens reflex cameras is to use extension rings; the trouble is that one is then tied to a fairly rigid scale of magnifications. Much more flexibility can be achieved by using either a special macro lens, or bellows. The latter method is clumsier, but has the advantage of extending the depth of focus. The roll-film camera I now use gives me a 6 × 6cm (2¼ × 2¼in) format and has built-in bellows that tilt. But more about its use later...

Choosing Slides or Prints

Undoubtedly it is best to choose colour slides rather than prints. For one thing one can tell immediately which pictures will accept enlargement, or be suitable for reproduction. The main criterion should be the sensitivity of the film emulsion, which in turn is related to its graininess; of lesser importance is the subjective impression of colour. As far as storage

---

* Often wrongly called macrophotography, which is the photography of large-scale objects.
† ASA (= American Standards Association) rating now being replaced by ISO (= International Standard Organisation).

of the slides is concerned, one needs to have some sort of system worked out from the start, for, by the time one has accumulated several hundred slides, sorting them out, or trying to find the ones required, can be very time-consuming. I arrange mine according to genera as well as listing them on computer, but a card index system would serve equally well.

Making the Best of the Subject

Let us now get down to photographing day lilies as such. Unlike painters, photographers are not able to idealise their subjects; they have to make the best of what they find. The photograph needs to serve both as a record, the scientific aspect as it were, and be aesthetically pleasing, i.e. of artistic merit. Consequently I often rearrange my subject to some extent with the help of florists' wire. There is a published picture of 'Lady Inara', for instance, where it is really quite impossible to tell that the distances of the flower scapes relative to one another, and thus the general shape of the plant has been 'favourably adjusted'. This should not be considered as cheating, since the eye does not always see objectively either. Similarly there is no harm in cutting away something in the foreground that happens to be in the way, or indeed in adding to the background.

Depth of Focus and Magnification

The closer one needs to get to the subject in close-up photography the greater the technical problems that need to be overcome. It is of course relatively easy to take a full-face shot of a day lily flower, but the effect is then rather flat, and furthermore the anthers will tend to be out of focus. It helps to try to angle the shot more, but this means having to decide what else should lie within the field of focus, so that the overall appearance of the photograph is clear and sharp. The problem can be surmounted by using a facility that most cameras now have. By pressing the manual stop-down lever the viewing screen will darken as the aperture adjusts to the pre-set working size and thus gives an impression of what is or is not in focus. Therefore set the shutter at $f8$ or $f11$ and then adjust the lens so that the foreground, at least, is in sharp focus. It does not matter if the background is slightly fuzzy; indeed it is sometimes better if it is, since the subject will then stand out more prominently.

If you happen to possess extension bellows with the facility to allow camera movements (the ability to alter the relative positions and angles of the lens and film planes) the field of focus can be adjusted with comparative ease. Even when the lens is open at its widest, it is possible to detect changes in sharpness from foreground to background depending on the inclination of the lens. In this way a satisfactory depth of field can be obtained even at fairly wide apertures ($f4$ to $f5.6$). By virtue of the fact that the camera lens is set at an angle to the film plane as well as to the subject, two blooms can be in sharp focus, although they are staggered one behind the other. For this the lens has to be tilted forward on the side nearer the closer flower.*

When photographing flowers

whose segments have a dark colour on the reverse side, such as 'Corky', it is necessary to introduce another bloom into the picture, so that the difference between the face and the side, or back view is clear. Profuse flowering can be indicated if one or two buds are shown in the picture as well as the actual flower. The difference between miniature and giant-flowered sorts can be made clear by including a number of the former in frame, if not the whole plant, for what appears smaller in a picture must surely also be smaller in nature.

A Camera Sees Things Differently

We need next to give thought to the question of the colour of the flower. It is well known that the colour quality of daylight varies during the course of a day: in the morning it is more yellow, at midday more blue and in the evening more red. There are also two periods of unbiased illumination, one at mid-morning and the other at mid-afternoon, when the lighting is neutral. If, therefore, one wants to intensify the blueness of a flower it is best to photograph it in the middle of the day, and any purple ones can be shot then, as well as in the evening. This is not a trick of any kind, but rather a way of reinforcing our subjective perception. If one wishes to photograph absolutely true colours, then one needs colour-temperature meters and a large selection of filters. And later the processing laboratory will quite likely eradicate all the hard work anyway!

White day lilies need special treatment so that they really do appear as white. Unbiased illumination is a must, and the light meter in the camera must be overriden. This is because it is normally set to give a mean value based on the totality of all the colours within the frame. If there is not a great deal of background, the resulting slide is thus liable to be underexposed. In such circumstances the aperture needs to be perhaps half a stop up, but it is probably best to take a series of shots each at a slightly different setting, since no two films are identical.

When one is photographing light-coloured flowers yet another effect can manifest itself. On the slide one suddenly notices a coloured mark similar to a spread-out yellow throat, which could not be seen with the naked eye. The colour sensitivity of the film emulsion resembles the colour spectrum that an insect registers. According to Thomas Barr, many *Hemerocallis* are night-blooming and rely on night-flying moths for pollination. I have often noticed the presence of hover flies, which seem to thrive on the nectar. Infra-red photography would probably reveal other flower signals aimed specifically at the insect population.

In the USA there is a series of awards for photographs of day lilies. One of these is the 'Robert Way Schlumpf Award', which is given for the best plant representation and the best garden picture. The 'A.D. Roquemore Memorial Award' requires not just a single bloom, but a picture of the entire day lily plant. And lastly there is also the prize

---

* The rule covering the setting of a technical camera with swing and tilt movements is known as the 'Scheimpflug Condition'.

for the best illustrated report, the 'Region 14 Sequence Award'.

Day Lilies on the Menu

Those readers who are 'into' Chinese food will take what follows for granted, though it may well seem a bit strange to the average European. Day lilies, either dried or fresh, are a normal ingredient in many Chinese dishes. Since all parts of the plant are edible, each has its own special use. The young shoots, for example, are cooked as a vegetable, though they have to be blanched first to remove the hallucinatory component. Then there are those species that form small tubers as a result of root constriction. These may be eaten raw in salads, or roasted like chestnuts; they taste a bit like radish, but not quite so sharp.

It is, however, chiefly the flowers and buds which are used in Asian cookery. Day lilies are as nutritious and vitamin-rich, if not more so, as any other vegetable (see table).

There may be a certain amount of prejudice against day lily flowers as a food, but perhaps we should take into account the fact that cauliflower and broccoli are also plants whose flowers are eaten. The additional advantage with day lilies is that with minimal attention these winter-hardy plants constantly throw out new shoots. How happy allotment holders would be if all their vegatables behaved in so exemplary a fashion! Any reader who has so far not knowingly eaten the flowers of day lilies, may wonder what they taste like. In simple terms one might just say that they taste of day lilies, that their taste is unique, but some people liken the taste to a mixture of green beans and mushrooms, while others think that it resembles asparagus. Since our sense of taste is very much connected with our sense of smell, fragrant day lilies are more likely to be described as sweet.

Day lilies may be harvested at any time during the flowering period. It is best to pick the buds on the day before they open, but some people prefer the flowers when these are at their peak. Like other vegetables, day lilies for the table can be deep frozen and so enjoyed all the year round. The day lilies should be blanched for three minutes and then rapidly chilled in cold water before being placed in the freezer cabinet. Often both buds and flowers are frozen simply because they are then more readily to hand. When the buds are put into boiling water they usually open up. If one wants to prevent

Protein and Vitamin Content of Day Lily Buds

Vegetable	Vitamin C mg/100 g	Vitamin A IU	Protein %
Day lily buds	43	983	3.1
Green beans	19	630	2.4
Asparagus	33	1000	2.2

this, it is best to pick the buds a few days before they would normally have opened.

It would not be right to concentrate wholly on theory, so here are some recipes for enterprising cooks.

Chicken with Day lily

1 chicken breast
1 onion
1 teaspoon ground ginger
salt and pepper
3 cups day lilies
1 teaspoon soy sauce
1 teaspoon starch flour
3 teaspoons oil (or fat)

Slice the chicken breast as thinly as possible and chop half the onion finely. Mix together the chicken, onion, pepper, soy sauce, ginger and flour. Fry quickly in some of the oil (or fat) for two minutes or so. Remove the meat from the pan and brown the rest of the onion, coarsely chopped, in the remaining oil. Next put in the day lily buds and pour on ¼ cup of water, adding salt to taste. Simmer gently and finally return the meat and allow to heat through again.

Day lily Soup

½kg pork belly strips, cubed
1.5l water
1 cup potato, cut into cubes
2 cups day lily buds
1 onion
salt and pepper
1 dessertspoon sherry
ginger

Briefly sear the pork with the chopped onion. Add the sherry, bring to the boil and then add the water. Now add the potatoes and season to taste; simmer gently for about one hour. Garnish with the day lilies and two or three pieces of ginger about five minutes before serving and maintain gentle heat until required.

Day lily Casserole

2 dozen *Hemerocallis* buds
2–4 rashers streaky bacon
2 onions
1 cup water
1 tin whole chestnuts
1 small tin mushrooms
1 tin cream of mushroom soup
salt and pepper

First fry the bacon until crisp; then remove rashers from pan and set aside. Slice the onions thinly and brown in the bacon fat. Add the water and salt and pepper to taste. Bring to the boil, add the *Hemerocallis* buds and allow to simmer gently to let them soften but not cook through. Next add the mushrooms and the chestnuts, either whole or chopped, and then fold in the cream of mushroom soup. Pour the mixture into a heated casserole dish, place the crispy bacon rashers on the top and continue to cook in a moderate oven for a short while.

Deepfried Day lilies

Coat about a dozen or so fresh or defrosted *Hemerocallis* buds with beaten egg, then sprinkle over a mixture of seasoned flour and garlic salt, and plunge them into hot oil until they are crisp.

Steamed Day lilies

Place the buds in a casserole dish or a flat pan and simmer gently in a little water. Do not overcook! When the water has boiled away, remove the buds from the pan, pour melted butter over them and sprinkle with garlic salt. Serve hot.

APPENDICES

Appendix I Societies

Addresses correct at time of publication but subject to alterations:

British Hosta and Hemerocallis Society
Membership Secretary: Mrs Elaine Elliott
  Jackdaws
  Back Lane
  Ingoldsby
  Grantham
  Lincs, NG33 4EW
Publications: *BHHS Bulletin*, published yearly, also two Newsletters per annum.
Activities: About one-third of the publications devoted to *Hemerocallis*, lectures and garden visits, information on plant sources.

American Hemerocallis Society
Correspondence: Elly Launius
  1454 Rebel Drive
  Jackson, Mississippi 39211
  USA
Publications: *The Day lily Journal* (formerly *The Hemerocallis Journal*), published quarterly, also *Checklist* annually and as collected volumes at intervals.
Activities: Devoted exclusively to *Hemerocallis*, maintains international register, slide sequences (on loan also for Europe), awards (see p. 94), lectures, special-interest sections (accessible to those not living in USA through the various round robins).

Gesellschaft der Staudenfreunde
(formerly Deutsche Iris- und Liliengesellschaft)
Correspondence: Martel Hald
  Dorrenklingenweg 35
  D-7114 Pfedelbach-Untersteinbach
  Federal Republic of Germany
Publications: *Der Staudengarten*, published quarterly.
Activities: Separate *Hemerocallis* specialist section meets annually, trials gardens with evaluation and awards, popularity list, seed exchanges.

Gesellschaft Schweizer Staudenfreunde
(formerly Schweizer Iris- und Lilienfreunde)
Correspondence: Marianne Lorenzi
  Lochackerstrasse 7
  CH-8302 Kloten
  Switzerland
Publications: *Schweizer Staudengartner*, published half-yearly.
Activities: Seed and plant exchanges, recommendation lists and individual advice, source lists for plants and supplies, excursions.

APPENDICES

Vlaamse Irisvereniging
Correspondence: Gilbert Verwijver
  Hogeweg 111
  B-2091 Hoevenen
  Belgium
Publications: *Iris*, published quarterly.
Activities: *Hemerocallis*, *Iris* and bulb plants share equal prominence, exchange of plants (sales through the society, which takes a proportion of the proceeds to defray costs), lectures and garden visits.

Australian Hemerocallis Society
Correspondence: Hon. Sec. Mrs Tricia
  Ryan Gonzales
  6 Lisle Street
  Tarragindi
  Queensland 4121
  Australia
Publications: *Journal of the Australian Hemerocallis Society* published yearly.
Activities: Meetings, cut-flower shows, display gardens, 'round robin'.

Appendix II
Hemerocallis Sources

Britain

Apple Court
Hordle Lane
Lymington
Hants, SO41 OHU

Bressingham Gardens
Diss
Norfolk, IP22 2AB

David Austin Roses
Bowling Green Lane
Albrighton
Wolverhampton, WV7 3HB

Goldbrook Plants
Hoxne, Eye
Suffolk, IP21 5AN

Kelways
Langport
Somerset, TA10 9SL

Mallorn Gardens
Lanner Hill
Redruth
Cornwall, TR16 6DA

Meare Close Nurseries
Tadworth Street
Tadworth
Surrey, KT20 5RQ

Perryhill Nurseries
Hartfield
East Sussex, TN7 4JP

Germany

Friesland Staudengarten
Uwe Knoepnadel
Husumerweg 16
2942 Jever 3

Schoeppinger Irisgarten
Werner Reinermann
Burgerweg 8
4437 Schoeppingen

Willumeit
Heidelberger Landstrasse 179
6100 Darmstadt-Eberstadt

Countess Zeppelin
7811 Sulzburg-Laufen

Belgium

François Verhaert
Fatimalaan 14
3343 Zandhoven

Jardinart-Van Mulders S.P.R.L.
Meerstraat 11
3018 Wijgmaal/Leuven

United States of America
It is possible to obtain day lilies direct from an exporter in the USA. There are 15 regions based on the geographic/climatic location of the various states.

Region 1:
none

Region 2:
John & Janet Benz, 12195 6th Avenue,
  Cincinnati, Ohio 42549

APPENDICES

Borbelata Gardens, 15974 Canby Avenue, Route 5, Faribault, Minnesota 55021

Hite Garden, 370 Gallogly Road, Pontiac, Michigan 48055

Illini Iris Garden, Rt. 3, Box 5, Monticello, Illinois 61856

Klehm's Nursery, Rt. 5, Box 197, Penny Road, South Barrington, Illinois 60010

Pinecliffe Day Lily Gardens, 6604 Scotsville Rd, Floyds Knobs, Indiana 47119

River Forest Nursery, 303 Fir Street, Michigan City, Indiana 46360

The Flower Ladies Garden, 1560 Johnson Road, Granite City, Illinois 62040

Region 3:

Boylan Gardens, 1 Venango Avenue, Cambridge Springs, Pennsylvania 16403

Forstlake Gardens, Box 535 LOW, Locust Grove, Virginia 22508

Hickory Hill Gardens, 1 Box 11, Loretta, Pennsylvania 15940

Nicholls Gardens, 4724 Angus Drive, Gainsville, Virginia 22065

Region 4:

Bloomingfields Farm, Gaylordsville, Connecticut 06755-0055

Lee Bristol Nursery, PO Box 5, Gaylordsville, Connecticut 06755

Floyd Cove Nursery, 11 Shipyard Lane, Setauket, New York 11733

Saxton Gardens, 1 First St., Saratoga Springs, New York 12866

Seawright Gardens, 134 Indian Hills, Carlisle, Maine 01741

Tranquil Lake Nursery Inc., 45 River St., Rehoboth, Maine 02769

Region 5:

Thundering Springs Day Lily Garden, PO Box 2013, Dublin, Georgia 31040

Region 6:

Albert G. Faggard, 3840 LeBleu St., Beaumont, Texas 77707

Bear Creek Farms, 16901 Loch Maree Nane, Houston, Texas 77084

Region 7:

Cordon Bleu Farms, PO Box 2033, San Marcos, California 929069

Greenwood Day Lily Gardens Inc., 4905 Pioneer 10, Whittier, California 90601

Melrose Gardens, 309 Best Road South, Stockton, California 95205

Region 8:

Caprice Farm Nursery, 15425 SW Pleasant Hill, Sherwood, Oregon 97140

Dr J.C. Halinar, 2334 Crooked Finger Rd., Scotts Mills, Oregon 97375

Wildwood Gardens, PO Box 250, Molalla, Oregon 97039-0250

Region 9:

none

Region 10:

Oakes Day Lilies, 8204 Monday Rd., Corryton, Tennessee 37721

Skyland Gardens, 4005 Skyland Drive, Kingsport, Tennessee 37664

Weir Gardens, Rt. 1, Box 99C, Kingston, Tennessee 37763

Region 11:

Adamgrove, Rt. 1, Box 246, California, Missouri 65018

American Day Lily & Perennials, PO Box 210, Grain Valley, Missouri 64029

Last Scent Farm, PO Box 100, Newcastle, Oklahoma 73065

River City Day Lilies, 779 Perry Avenue, Cape Girardeau, Missouri 63701

S. & M. Smith, 501 Bourne Avenue, Columbia, Missouri 65203

Gilbert H. Wild, 1112 Joplin St., Sarcoxie, Missouri 64862-0338

Region 12:

Corner Oaks Garden, 6139 Blanding Blvd., Jacksonville, Forida 32244

Day Lily Discounters, Rt. 2, Box 24, Dept. S.L., Alachua, Florida 32615

Day Lily World, PO Box 1612, Sanford, Florida 32771-1612

Rollingwood Gardens, PO Box 1044, Eustis, Florida 32727

Wimberley Way Gardens, 7024 NW 18th Avenue, Gainsville, Florida 32605

Region 13:
Crochet Day Lily Garden, PO Box 425, Prairieville, Louisiana 70769
Guidry's Day Lily Garden, 1005 E Vermilion St, Abbeville, Louisiana 70510
Hobby Garden, 38164 Monticello Drive, Prairieville, Louisiana 70769
Louisiana Nursery, Rt. 7, Box 43, Opelousas, Louisiana 70570

Region 14:
Galloway Gardens, 3412 Galloway, Jackson, Mississippi 39216
Mayos Day Lilies, Rt. 2, Box 255, Reform, Alabama 35481
McCrae's Hilltop Garden, Rt. 5, Box 65, Hamilton, Alabama 35570
Twin Pines Day Lily Garden, 4743 Dubarry La., Jackson, Mississippi 39209

Region 15:
Meadowlake Gardens, Rt. 4, Box 709, Walterboro, S Carolina 29488
Oxford Gardens, 3022 Oxford Dr., Durham, N Carolina 27707
Powell's Gardens, Rt. 3, Box 21, Princeton, N Carolina 27569
Renaissance Garden, 1047 Baron Rd., Weddington, N Carolina 28173

Roycroft Nursery & Landscaping, 305 Egret Circle, Georgetown, S Carolina 29440

Australia

New South Wales:
Rainbow Ridge Nursery (Graeme and Helen Grosvenor and John Taylor), 8 Taylors Rd, Dural 2158

Victoria:
Tempo Two Nursery (Barry and Lesley Blyth), 57–59 East Rd, Pearcedale 3912

Queensland:
Daylily Display Centre (M. Flanders and M. Mead), Tirroan, Gin Gin 4671
Mountain View Daylily Nursery (Scott Alexander), McCarthy's Rd, Maleny 4552
K. Simpson, 39 Amega St, Mt Gravatt 4122
Wyamba Gardens (Mr & Mrs J. Agnew), 33 Woodford Rd, Pullenvale 4069

Tasmania:
Woolnorth Station (K. & L. Else), Montagu Via Smithton 7330

Western Australia:
Iris-Daylily Display Gardens, Lot 141 Great Northern Hwy, Bullsbrook 6084

Appendix III
First Descriptions of *Hemerocallis* Species

Botanical Name	Common Name	Author and Source
H. altissima	(Tall Day Lily)	Stout, *Herbertia* 1943, 9:103
H. aurantiaca	(Orange-Fulvous) or (Summer Day Lily)	Baker, *Gardeners' Chronicle* 1890, III:8:94
H. aurantiaca var. *littorea*		Nakai, *Bot.Mag.* Tokyo 1 46:111–123
H. aurantiaca	'Major'	Baker, *Gardeners' Chronicle* 1895, III:18:62
H. × *baroni*		Sprenger, *Gardeners' Chronicle* 1903, 34:122
H. citrina	(Long Yellow) or (Citron Day Lily)	Baroni, *Nuov.Giorn.Bot.Ital.* 1897, II:4:305
H. citrina var. *vespertina*		[(Hara) Erhardt 1988]

APPENDICES

H. coreana	(Korean Day Lily)	Nakai, *Bot.Mag.* Tokyo 1932, 46:123
H. crocea		Lamarch, Pl.Fr. 1799; 3:267
H. darrowiana		Hu, *Hemerocallis Journal* 1969, 4:26
H. disticha		Donahue and David Prod. Florae Nepalensis 1825
H. dumortieri	(Dumortier's Day Lily)	Morren, *Hort.Belg.* 1834, 2:195, pl.43
H. × *elmensis*		Sprenger, *Gardeners' Chronicle* 1903, 34:122
H. esculenta		Koidzumi, *Bot.Mag.* Tokyo 1925, 39:28
H. exaltata		Stout, *Addisonia* 1934, 18:27, t.595
H. forrestii	(Forrest's Day Lily)	Diels, *Notes Bot. Gard. Edin.* 1912, 5:198
H. fulva	(Fulvous or Tawny Day Lily)	Linnaeus, *Species Plantarum* ed. 1762 2:462
H. fulva var. *angustifolia*		Baker, *Linn.Soc.Bot* 1871, 11:359
H. fulva var. *disticha*		Baker, *Jour.Brit.* For. 1874, 12
H. fulva var. *longituba*		Maximowicz, *Gartenflora* 1885, 34
H. fulva var. *pauciflora*		Hotta and Matsuoka, *Acta Phytotax. Geobot.* 1966, 22:1
H. fulva var. *rosea*		Stout, *Addisonia* 1930, 15:t.484
H. fulva var. *sempervirens*		Hotta and Matsuoka *Acta.Phytotax.Geobot.* 1966, 22:42
H. graminea		Andrews, *Bot.Repros* 1802, 4:pl.244
H. hakunensis		Nakai, *Jour.Jap.Bot.* 1943, 19:315
H. × *hippeastroides*		Sprenger, *Gardeners' Chronicle* 1908, 54:122
H. lilioasphodelus	(Lemon or Tall Yellow or Custard Day Lily)	Linnaeus emend. Hylander, *Sp.Pl.* 1753, 324
H. longituba		Miquel, *Ann.Mus.Bot.Ludg.* 1867, 3:152
H. lutea		Gaertner, Fruct. 1790, 2:15
H. × *luteola*		Jenkins, *Garden* 1900, 57:407
H. micrantha		Nakai, *Jour. Jap.Bot.* 1943, 19:315
H. middendorffii	(Amur or Middendorff's Day Lily)	Trautvetter et Meyer Middend. Reise 1856, 2:94
H. minor	(Grass-leaved or Star Day Lily)	Miller, *Gardeners' Dict.* ed. 1768, 8
H. × *muelleri*		Sprenger, *Gardeners' Chronicle* 1903, 90:151
H. multiflora		Stout, Addisonia 1929, 14:31, t.464
H. nana	(Dwarf Day Lily)	Smith et Forrest, *Notes Bot.Gard.Edin* 1916, 10:39
H. × *ochroleuca*		Sprenger, *Gardeners' Chronicle* 1903, 34:122
H. pedicellata		Nakai, *Bot.Mag.Tokyo* 1932, 46:117

H. plicata	Stapf, *Bot.Mag.* 1923 T.8968
H. sulphurea	Nakai, *Bot.Mag.Tokyo* 1932, 46:121
H. thunbergii (Thunberg's or Late Yellow Day Lily)	Barr emend. Baker, *Gardeners' Chronicle* 1890, III 8:94
H. vespertina	Hara, *Jour.Jap.Bot.* 1941, 17:127
H. × *vomerensis*	Sprenger, *Gardeners' Chronicle* 1903, 34:122
H. washingtoniana	Traub, *Plant Life* 1951, vol. VII
H. yezoensis	Hara, *Jour.Jap.Bot.* 1937, 14:250

Appendix IV
Excluded Names

Hemerocallis alba (Andrews 1801) = *Hosta plantaginea* [(Lam.) Ascherson]

H. albomarginata (Hort.ex Vilmorin 1865) = *Hosta sieboldii* [(Baxt.) Ingram]

H. caerulea (Andrews 1797) = *Hosta ventricosa* [(Salisb.) Stearn]

H. chinensis (Hort.ex Steudel 1821) = *Hosta sieboldiana* [(Hook.) Engler]

H. cordifolia (Thunberg 1784) = *Cardiocrinum cordatum* [(Thunb.) Makino]

H. japonica (Thunberg 1784) = *Hosta lancifolia* [(Thunb.) Engler]

H. japonica (Thunberg 1794) = *Hosta sieboldiana* [(Hook.) Engler]

H. japonica (Redouté 1802) = *Hosta plantaginea* [(Lam.) Ascherson]

H. lancifolia (Thunberg 1802) = *Hosta lancifolia* [(Thunb.) Engler]

H. liliastrum (Linnaeus 1753) = *Paradisea liliastrum* [(L.) Bertolini]

H. plantaginea (Lamarck 1789) = *Hosta plantaginea* [(Lam.) Ascherson]

H. sieboldiana (Loddiges 1832) = *Hosta sieboldiana* [(Hook.) Engler]

H. speciosa (Sweet 1830) = *Hymenocallis speciosa* (L.f. ex Salisbury)

H. undulata [(Sieb.) Bailey] = *Hosta undulata* [(Otto et A. Dietr.) Bailey]

BIBLIOGRAPHY

Books

American Hemerocallis Society (AHS): *Day Lilies – Beginner's Handbook 1978*.
AHS: *Checklist 1957*
AHS: *Checklist 1973*
AHS: *Checklist 1983*
Corliss, P.G.: *Hemerocallis – The Perennial Supreme*. The Aucune Press, San Francisco 1951.
Dahlgren and Clifford: *The Monocotyledons: A comparative study*. Academic Press, London/New York 1982.
Dahlgren, Clifford and Yeo: *The Families of the Monocotyledons*. Springer Verlag, Berlin/New York 1985.
Darrow, G.M. and Meyer, F.G. (Publisher): *Day Lily Handbook*. The American Horticultural Magazine, Volume 47, Number 2, 1968.
Davis, B.A.: *Day Lilies and how to grow them*. Tupper and Love, Atlanta 1954.
Encke, F., Buchheim, G. and Seybold, S.: *Zander – Hand-worterbuch der Pflanzennamen*. Verlag Eugen Ulmer, Stuttgart 1984.
Koehlein, F. *Pflanzen vermehren leicht gemacht*. Verlag Eugen Ulmer, Stuttgart 1975.
Munson, R.W., Jr.: *Hemerocallis, The Day Lily*. Timber Press, Portland, Oregon 1989.
Stout, A.B.: *Day Lilies*. The Macmillan Company, New York 1934. (Reprint 1986)

Periodicals/Journals

(Articles that are simply listings without descriptions are not included.)
Allgood, J.M.: 'Awards for 1978'. *Hemerocallis Journal*, 1978, vol.4, 17ff.
'Evergreens flourish in North'. *Day Lily Journal*, 1981, vol.3, 49ff.
'Hybridizing can be fun'. *Day Lily Journal*, 1982, vol.4, 53ff.
'The little ones are here to stay'. *Hemerocallis Journal*, 1980, vol.2, 11ff.
'The wonderful world of color'. *Hemerocallis Journal*, 1980, vol.4, 30ff.
Barr, T.C.: 'Hemerocallis and the new plant biosystematics'. *Day Lily Journal* vol. 42, no. 2, 66ff.
Barr, T.C. i.a.: 'The evolution of red tetraploid *Hemerocallis*'. *Day Lily Journal*, 1985, vol.4, 317ff.
Bottling, P.: 'Germination of diploid day lily seeds'. *Hemerocallis Journal*, 1974, vol. 2, translated by T. Maier for Staudengarten 1976.
Brockington, P.: 'Jablonsky shares experiences'. *Day Lily Journal*, 1982, vol.4, 22ff.
Burns, L.: 'Spiders dazzle viewers'. *Day Lily Journal*, 1984, vol.4, 361ff.
'What is a spider?' *Day Lily Journal*, 1985, vol.3, 243ff.
Busse, A.: 'Landscaping with day lilies: Philosophy . . .' *Day Lily Journal*, 1985, vol.3, 272ff.
Cerchione, A.J.: 'Catalogs – the link between buyer and seller'. *Day Lily Journal*, 1985, vol.3, 265ff.

'Photography – the promise and the problems'. *Day Lily Journal*, 1986, vol.3, 312ff.

Chappel, G.W.: 'Use color wisely'. *Day Lily Journal*, 1983, vol.3, 56ff.

Coe, F.W.: 'The *Hemerocallis* Species'. *Hemerocallis Yearbook*, 1958, 152ff.

Darrow, G.M.: '*Hemerocallis aurantiaca* littorea and its use in breeding'. *Hemerocallis Journal*, 1943, vol.1, 23ff.

Dunbar, C.: 'Growing day lilies in containers'. *Day Lily Journal*, 1984, vol.2, 169ff.

Duvall, M.: 'Landscaping – some useful ideas'. *Day Lily Journal*, 1982, vol.3, 24ff.

Elliott, R.: 'Hybridizing – unlocking unseen dimensions'. *Day Lily Journal*, 1984, vol.4, 332ff.

'Lambert believes Blue Day Lily getting nearer'. *Newsletter Region 14*, Spring 1985.

Elliott, R.D.: 'Breeding for red, going for gold'. *Day Lily Journal*, 1985, vol.1, 41ff.

Fagard, A.C.: 'Double up and catch up'. *Hemerocallis Journal*, 1980, vol.4, 25ff.

Farr Nursery: 'The story behind and about Dr Stout's day lilies'. *Newsletter Region 13*, Summer 1984, 18.

Fischer, H.: 'Day lilies in Japan'. *Hemerocallis Journal*, 1979, vol.3, 53ff.

Hale, B.: 'Photographing day lilies'. *Hemerocallis Journal*, 1980, vol.2, 29ff.

Halinar, J.C.: 'The blue day lily – is it really so simple?' *Day Lily Journal*, 1984, vol.4, 337ff.

Hart, M.B.: 'Notes of day lily tolerance of salt water'. *Hemerocallis Journal*, 1979, vol.2, 20ff.

Hu, S.: 'Exploration for new day lilies in S.Korea and Japan'. *Hemerocallis Journal*, 1969, vol.4, 12ff.

Irish, N.: 'What the rots questionaires told us'. *Hemerocallis Journal*, 1980, vol.1, 38ff.

Johnson, T.: 'What makes up our soil?' *Day Lily Journal*, 1983, vol.1, 25ff.

Johnson, W.: 'How do we judge in gardens?' *Day Lily Journal*, 1983, vol.3, 24ff.

Kasha, M. i.a.: 'Is the blue day lily near?' *Day Lily Journal*, 1982, vol.2, 68ff.

Kasha, M.: 'How to use the Lanoline-BAP-IAA paste'. *Day Lily Journal*, 1983, vol.1, 23ff.

'Hybridizing for a blue day lily – a response'. *Day Lily Journal*, 1984, vol.4, 341ff.

'New insights for the *Hemerocallis* hybridizer'. *Hemerocallis Journal*, 1978, vol.4, 45ff.

King, W.: 'Early history of AHS'. *Hemerocallis Journal*, 1980, vol.3, 54ff.

Kirby-Smith and Kasha: 'Propagation of *Hemerocallis* off-shoots'. *Day Lily Journal*, 1981, vol.4, 90ff.

Kitchingman, R.M.: 'Some species and cultivars of *Hemerocallis*'. *The Plantsman* 1985/86, 2, 68ff.

Krikorian and Kann: 'Mass blooming of a day lily clone'. *Hemerocallis Journal*, 1980, vol.1, 35ff.

Kroll, A.M.: 'Famous or forgotten?' *Day Lily Journal*, 1985, vol.3, 220ff.

Kuesel, H.B.: 'The flower bumble beetle'. *Hemerocallis Journal*, 1980, vol.1, 41ff.

Kurzmann, F.: 'Interessante Vermehrungsversuche mit Tag-lilien'. *Staudengarten*, 1975, vol.4, 22.

Lambert, J.R.: 'Fragrance in modern *Hemerocallis*'. *Hemerocallis Journal*, 1979, vol.4, 6ff.

Lankart, E.: 'What makes good parents?' *Day Lily Journal*, 1983, vol.2, 50ff.

Llanes, A.R.: 'Understanding plant diseases'. *Hemerocallis Journal*, 1979, vol.4, 43ff.

Matsuoka, M.: 'Wild *Hemerocallis* in Japan'. *Hemerocallis Journal*, 1963, vol.3, 38ff.

McCrone, H.: 'Is there a perfect miniature?' *Day Lily Journal*, 1985, vol.2, 127ff.

Mercer, R.: 'Pictorial essay'. *Day Lily Journal*, 1986, vol.2, 217ff.

Meyer, M.M.: 'Rapid propagation of *Hemerocallis* by tissue culture'. *Hemerocallis Journal*, 1979, vol.3, 20ff.

Mueller, W.: 'Erinnerungen an die ersten

BIBLIOGRAPHY

Hemerocallis-Zuechtungen in Neapel'. *DILG Jahrbuch* 1962/63, 139ff.

'Erinnerungen an meine Zeit in Neapel und Nocera Inferiore'. *DILG Jahrbuch* 1967, vol.1, 71ff.

Munson, B.: 'Milestones in twenty years . . ,' *Day Lily Journal*, 1984, vol.1, 12ff.

Orndorff, C.: 'Cultural and aesthetic values of garden mulching'. *Hemerocallis Journal*, 1981, vol.1, 22ff. 'Re-propagation of day lilies'. *Hemerocallis Journal*, 1981, vol.2, 25ff.

Peck, V.L.: 'Will we soon have ruffles and ruffles in all colors?' *Day Lily Journal*, 1982, vol.1, 48ff.

Pittard, C.M.: 'The root cuttage method of plant multiplication'. *Newsletter Region 3*, September 1983, 6.

Sellers, V.: 'Day lily deaths'. *Hemerocallis Journal*, 1979 vol.2, 18ff.

Simpson, D.: 'A winter protection idea . . .' *Day Lily Journal*, 1984, vol.3, 261ff.

Smith, M.G.: 'Thoughts for flower show judges'. *Hemerocallis Journal*, 1979, vol.2, 6ff.

Spencer, J.A.: 'Day lily rot: a recurring nemesis'. *Day Lily Journal*, 1985, vol.3, 238ff.

Stoutemeyer, V.: 'Organic horticulture'. *Hemerocallis Journal*, 1981, vol.2, 26ff.

Viette, A.: 'Can evergreens survive in a real gardening world?' *Day Lily Journal*, 1985, vol.3, 256ff.

Wallace, M.: 'Scape conversion'. *Day Lily Journal*, 1984, vol.1, 112ff.

Wollard, P.D.: 'Apomixis experiments fail'. *Day Lily Journal*, 1985, vol.2, 171ff.

Zahler, E.: 'How should we feed our day lilies?' *Newsletter Region 14*, Spring 1985, 9ff.

GENERAL INDEX

Figures in **bold** indicate black and white illustrations.

A.D. Roquemore Memorial Award 139
abscission method of germination **107**
America (USA)
  awards 22, 94–7, 135, 139–40
  breeders 21–2, 25
  early introductions 21
  societies 13, 21–2, 143, 144
American Hemerocallis Society 13, 74, 108, 117, 143
  awards 94–7
  breeding projects 102
  origins (1946) 21–2
Anderson, Mary 21–2
Annie T. Giles Award 96
anthers **30**, 31, 64
anthocyanidin pigments 103, 104
aphid damage 128–9
Apple Court Day Lily Display Garden 26
Australian Hemerocallis Society 26
azalea type 65

bacterial soft rot 127
banded flower patterns 63, 91–4
Barr, Peter 26
Belgium collection 26, 144

Berlin Trophy 112
BHHS *see* British Hosta and Hemerocallis Society
blue-toned varieties 87–91
botrytis (leaf spot) 127–8
bracts, description 30
branching flowers habit 70
breeders 21–6
breeding
  see also hybridisation
  pigments 103–5
  pollination/fertilisation 98–102, **101**
  special projects 102–5
Britain 20, 23–6
British Hosta and Hemerocallis Society 26, 73, 74, 91, 108, 143
Brummitt, Leonard 25
Buck, W.Q. 72

carotenoid pigments 103, 104
Cave, Leslie 26
Cercosphera hemerocallis 17
China **16**, 20, 23
  culinary uses 15, 16, 17, 140–2
  early writings 15, 16, 17
  medical uses 15, 16
  types 16–17
chromosome types 71–2
Citrina group 32
classification 21, 28–9, 31–2
climate tolerance 70–1, 80
Clusius (Ecluse) 17–19

Coe, Phillip 26
Coe, Robert 25–6
colchicine use 71–2
collotrichum (leaf spot) 127–8
colours
  flower patterns 61–5, **62**, **64**
  pigments 103–5, **104**
companion plants (list) 132, 133–5
Contarinia quinquenotata 128
cookery recipes 140–2
Cooper, Gordon 26
Countess von Zeppelin Nursery 84
crown, description 29
crown division 114–15, **115**
crown rot disease 126–7
cultivation 120–9
  companion plants (list) 133–5
  diseases/pests 126–9
  garden environment 130–5
  hybrid seedlings 104–6
  plant management 123–6
  plant sources 120, 144–6
  planting/sites 120–3, **121**, 130–3
Cypriani, Father 23

dead-heading 126
diamond dusting effect 60, 103

diploid types 71–2
diseases 126–8
diurnal flowers 68
Dodonaeus (Dodoens) 17, **18**, 19
Don Stevens Memorial Award 97
Donn Fischer Memorial Cup 95–6
dormancy 70–1, 121
dotting character 61
double flowers 65
dusting characters 60

Easton, Dandy, Perry's stock 25
enhancement patterns 91–4
Epsom and Ewell Parks Department collection 26
Europe 18, 19, 20–1
  16th century illustrations **18**
  20th century developments 22
  hybridisers 22–6
  registered hybrids 109–12
evergreen types 70, 71

Fay, Orville 25
feeding 124, 126
fertilisation **99**, 99–101
fertiliser application 125–6
Fischer, Hubert 25
Fisher, Helen Field 21–2
flavone co-pigments 103, 104
flavonoids 60
flavonol co-pigments 103, 104
floral art **135–6**, 136–8
flowers
  colours 31, 61–5, **62**, 64
  shapes 65–8, **66**
  sizes 68, 70, 72
  stripes **64**, 64–5
  structure **30**, 30–1
  timing/season 31, 68–9
foliage, description 29, **30**
food values 140
Frankliniella hemerocallis 129
frost protection 122

Fulva group 32

gall fly 128
garden environment 130–5
Germany 22–3, 26, 112, 143, 144
Gesellschaft der Staudenfreunde 74, 143
Gesellschaft Schweizer Staudenfreunde 143
Giraldi, Father 23
gold dusting effect 60
growth habits 69–71
  species compared **34–5**, **46–7**, **51**

habit *see* growth habits
halo flower patterns 63, 91–4
hardiness 70–1, 80
Hemerocallidaceae 28
hemerocallis fly 126, **128**
hemerocallis gall fly **128**
Hemerocallis Society 22
hemerocallis thrips **128**, 129
Henry Field Seed Company 21, 22
Henry, Pauline 91, 102
historic varieties 75–6, 80–1, 84–5, 88, 92
history 15–27
Hortus Vomerensis *see* Vomero
hose-in-hose double flower 65
hybridisation 98–112
  colour pigments 103–5, **104**
  cultivation 106
  evaluation chart **109**
  miniature varieties 102–3
  naming rules 109
  parental choice 98–9, 102
  record-keeping 101
  Registration 108–9
  seed management 105–7
  seedling selection 107–8
hybrids 60–97

Ida Munson Award 96
identification key 32–5
International Day Lily Register 109

James E. Marsh Award 97

Karl Foerster Medal 112
Kasha, M. 104, 117
Kirby-Smith, J.S. 117
Koehlein, Fritz 100
Kurzmann, Professor F. 114

L. Ernest Plouf CVFH Award 97
Ladham, Ernest 26
Lanoline-BAP-IAA propagation 116–18
large-flowered varieties 68, 76–8, 81–2, 85–6, 89–90, 92–3
layer-on-layer double flower 65
leaf characteristics 29, **30**, 69–71
leaf spots 126, 127–8
Leeds Parks Department collection 26
Lenington All-American Award 95
lily structure comparison 28
line breeding 99
Linnaeus (Linné) 17, 19
Little Hermitage (IofW) Collection 26
Lobelius (Lobel) 17, **18**

Mabel Y. Yaste Award 135
mail order suppliers 120, 144–6
Meyer, M.M. 118–19
Middendorffii group 32
midrib feature **64**, 64–5
Midwest Hemerocallis Society 22
miniature-flowered varieties 68, 79, 83, 87, 91, 94, 102–3
morphology 29–31, **30**
The Most Beautiful and Best Hemerocallis of Central Europe 112

GENERAL INDEX

mould prevention 126
mulches 124–5
Müller, Willy 21, 22–3
Multiflora group 32
Munson, R.W. 91
Mygus hemerocallis 128

names 109, 148
Nana group 32
National Hemerocallis Reference Collections 26
National Reference Collection (IoW) 91
near-white varieties 87–91
nematodes 129
New Zealand 27
nitrogen requirements 124, 125–6
nocturnal flowers 68
Northern Horticultural Society 73
Norton Hall Nursery 25, 84
nursery suppliers 120, 144–6

orchid-shaped flowers 67
ovary, structure 31
over-wintering feature 70–1, 80

paeony type 65
Palmengarten Medals 112
patterning 61–3, 91
perianth 30, **31**
Perry, Amos 24–5
Perry's Diary (Perry) 24
pests 126, **128**, 128–9
petals (tepals) 30, **31**
  colour distribution 61
  median stripes 64–5
  texture 67–8
phosphorus requirements 125–6
photography 136–40
picotee pattern effect 63
pink hybrids 83–7
pistil, structure 31
Pittard, C.M. 115
plant care 125–6
planting 120–2, **121**
pointed segments 67
pollen 31
pollination 98–102, **99**

parent plants 98–100
pollen storage 100–1
  records 101
  technique 99–101
polychrome flower colours 61
potassium requirements 125–6
proliferations 30, 115–16, **116**
propagation
  floral (hybrids) 98–112
  vegetative 113–19, **114–16**
protein content 140
pseudobulbs 29

Randall, Harry 25
recipes 140–2
red day lilies 19, 80–3
Region 14 Sequence Award 140
Registration, hybrids 108–9
reproductive organs **30**, 31
rhizoctonia (soft rot) 127
Richard C. Peck Award 97
Robert P. Miller Memorial Award 96
Robert Way Schlumpf Award 139
root division 113–14, **114**
roots 28, 29, **121**, 121–2
Royal Botanical Gardens, Kew 73
Royal Horticultural Society 73, 91, 108

scape 29–30, 31, 69–71
Schreiner, R. 72
seed capsule 31
seeds, description 28, 31
semi-evergreen types 70–1
sepals (tepals) 30
  colour distribution 61
  median stripes 64–5
  texture 68
Shenandoah, Iowa, Show (1946) 22
Siloam Springs Nursery, Arkansas 91
siting 122–3, 130–3
size comparisons **34–5**, **46–7, 51**

slugs 126, 129
small-flowered 68, 70, 78–9, 82–3, 86–7, 90, 93
snails 126, 129
society addresses (Appendix I) 143–4
soil conditions 122–3, 125
species 28–59
  classification 31–2
  growth habits **34–5**, **46–7, 51**
  identification key 32–5
  physical characteristics 29–31
Sprenger, Charles (Karl Ludwig) 21, 22–3
spring sickness 127
stamen structure 31
Steiger, Max 23, 26, 110
sterility studies 23
stigma 31
stipes **64**, 64–5
Stout, Dr Arlow B. 21
Stout Medal 22, 74, 94–5

tepals (petals/sepals) 30
tetraploid types 71–2, 103–4
thrip damage **128**, 129
throat colour, flowers 63–4, **64**
Thunberg, Carl Peter 20
time effects 68–9, **121**, 121–2
tip flower patterns 63, **64**
tissue culture propagation 118–19
Traub, H.P. 72
Tricolor Trophy 135
triploid types 71
tub culture 123

varieties 75–97
  awards 94–7
  choosing 73–4, 120, 123
  enhancement patterns 91–4
  pink and related tones 83–7
  red shades 80–3
  white and blue tones 87–91
  yellow types 74–80
veins, prominence 64

154

Verhaert, François 26
vitamins 140
Vlaamse Irisvereniging, Belgium 26
Vomero (Hortus Vomerensis) 22, 23

Wallace, R. 26

watering 123–4
watermark flower patterns 63, 91–4
weed control 126
whiteness factor 104
 see also near-white varieties
Wimberley Way Gardens, Florida 91
Wisley RHS garden 91

Yeld, George 23–4
yellow-flowered 19, 74–9

Zandhoven, Belgium collection 27, 144

INDEX OF SPECIES, VARIETIES AND HYBRIDS

Figures in **bold** refer to black and white illustrations. *See also* list of first descriptions in Appendix III on pages 146–7 and excluded species in Appendix IV on page 148.

'Acadiana Snow' 104
'Agape Love' 89
'Age of Chivalry' 105
'Ajax' 23
'Alan' 80
altissima 16
    characteristics 29, 30
    classification 32
    description 25–6, **36**
    fragrance 132–3
    identification 33
    introduction date 59
'Amadeus' 80, 81
'American Revolution' 81
'Amersham' 25
'Amos Perry' 24
'Angel Artistry' 93
'Ann Blocher' 63
'Anzak' 132
'Apollo 17' 110
'Apple Court Damson' 89
'Apple Crisp' 76
'Apple Tart' 80, 81, 97
'Apricot' 24, 75
'Apricot Angel' 84, 95
Asphodelum 18
Asphodelus liliaceus luteus 19
    rubens 19

Asphodelus luteus liliflorus 28
'Astolat' 89, 96
'Aten' 75
'August Orange' 21, 75
aurantiaca 21, 24
    classification 32
    description 36–7, **37**
    growth habit **47**
    identification 33
    introduction date 59
    'Major' 23, 32, 37–8, 52
    var. *littorea* 37, 48
'Autumn' 86, 97
'Ava Michelle' 75, 95

'Bald Eagle' 81
'Bambi Doll' 84, 96
'Banbury Canary' 25
'Banbury Cinnamon' 25, 75
'Banbury Contrast' 92
'Banbury Signal' 80
'Barbary Corsair' 90
× *baroni* 23, 38
'Bayreuther Phoenix' 110
'Beauty' *see* 'Sovereign'
'Becky Lynn' 85, 95
'Benchmark' 89
'Berggarten' 110
'Berlin Circle' 110
'Berlin Giant' 110
'Berlin Lavender' 110
'Berlin Multi' 110
'Berlin Oxblood' 110
'Berlin Red' 110
'Berlin Red Star' 110
'Berlin Red Velvet' 110

'Berlin Trophy' 112
'Berlin Watermelon' 110
'Berliner Anfang' 110
'Berliner Mondlicht' 110
'Berliner Premiere' 69, 110
'Berliner Zimtstaub' 110
'Bernard Thompson' 76
'Bertie Ferris' 79, 95
'Bess Ross' 26, 80, 95
'Bette Davis Eyes' 92, 97
'Betty Woods' 65, 76, 95, 96
'Bitsy' 79, 95, 132
'Blanco Real' 89, 96
'Blue Bristol' 104
'Blue Happiness' 85
'Blushing Maiden' 86
'Bonanza' 92
'Bourbon Kings' 80
'Brent Gabriel' 89
'Bright Spangles' 76
'Brilliant Glow' 72
'Brocaded Gown' 76, 95
'Brunhild' 110
'Bruno Muller' 26, 81
'Buffy's Doll' 93, 96
'Bumble Bee' 94
'Burning Daylight' 76
'Butterpat' 79, 96
'Butterscotch Ruffles' 78
'Button Box' 90
'Buzz Bomb' 26, 80
'By Myself' 76, 116
'Byng of Vimy' 24

'Cabbage Flower' 76, 96
'Cadence' 84
'Cajun Caprice' 105

INDEX OF SPECIES, VARIETIES AND HYBRIDS

'Cajun Gambler' 76
'Call to Remembrance' 89, 104
'Camden Gold Dollar' 78
'Cartwheels' 65, 75, 77, 95
'Catherine Woodbery' 88, 104
'Celestial Light' 105
'Cenla Triumph' 85
'Chateau Blanc' 96
'Cherry Cheeks' 81
'Cherry Ripe' 25, 80
'Chestnut Lane' 77
'Chicago' 89
'Chicago Apache' 81
'Chicago Cameo' 85
'Chicago Knobby' 89, 97
'Chicago Picotee Memories' 63
'Chicago Queen' 89
'Chicago Royal' 105
'Chicago Royal Robe' 89
'Chicago Ruby' 81
'Chicago Sunrise' 77
'Chinese Autumn' 77
'Chinese Temple Flower' 92
'Chingford' 24
'Chorus Line' 87, 96, 97
'Chosen One' 104
'Christmas Carol' 80
'Christmas Is' 82
'Chrysolite' 24
'Cindy Marie' 83, 85
citrina 16, 20–1, 23, 24
   characteristics 29, 68
   classification 32
   description **38**, 38–9
   growth habit **35**
   identification 33
   introduction date 59
   var. *vespertina* 39
'Clarence Simon' 85, 95
Colchium autumnale 71–2
'Color Splash' 104
'Colour Me Yellow' 77
'Coming Your Way' 85
'Condilla' 77, 95, 96
coreana 32, 33, **39**, 40, 59
'Corky' 26, 75, 79, 95, 132, 139
'Corsican Bandit' 93
'Cosmic Hummingbird' 93
'Cranberry Baby' 82
'Creamy Egret' 105

'Cressida' 72
'Crimson Icon' 82
'Crimson Pirate' 80
crocea 40, 46
'Crown Royal' 97
'Curls' 79, 95

'Daily Bread' 79
'Dainty Dreamer' 87
'Dance Ballerina Dance' 83, 98
'Dancing Shiva' 85, 97
'Dark Elf' 90
'Darrell' 77
darrowiana 29, 32, **40**, **51**
'Dauntless' 21, 75, 94
'David Paul French' 78
'Dawn Delight' 105
'Dawn Piper' 81
'Dewey Roquemore' 81
'Dixie Land' 92
'Dorethe Louise' 77
'Dorothy McDade' 75
'Double Bourbon' 96
'Double Cutie' 78, 96
'Double Flash-Splash' 82
'Double Grapette' 89
'Double Honey' 75
'Double Razzle Dazzle' 82, 96
'Douglas Dale' 82, 97
dumortieri 21, 23–4
   border sites 133
   characteristics 29, 30
   classification 32
   description 40–1, **41**
   growth habit **47**
   introduction date 59

'E.A. Bowles' 24
'Ed Murray' 70, 82, 95, 96
'Edna Spalding' 84
'Eenie Allegro' 78, 133
'Eenie Fanfare' 83, 133
'Eenie Weenie' 78, 133
'Egyptian Spice' 85
'Eidelweiss' 77
'Elaine Strutt' 25–6, 84
'Elfriede' 110
'Elizabeth Anne Hudson' 92
'Elizabeth Yancey' 85, 118
'Ellen Christine' 77
× *elmensis* 23
'Elsie Kearney' 88

Emerocallis **17**
'Empress Seal' 72, 89
'Enchanter's Spell' 96
esculenta 17, 32, 34, 41, **42**, 59
'Estmere' 24
'Etched in Gold' 85
'Evening Bell' 97
'Everblooming Doll' 78
exaltata 32, **34**, **42**, 43, 59
exilis (= *exaltata*) 43

'Fairy Frosting' 87
'Fairy Tale Pink' 83, 85, 95
'Fairy Wings' 75, 95
'Family Portrait' 105
'Fanny Stadler' 82
'Fashion Delight' 113
'Feuervogel' 26
'Finest Hour' 26
'Fingal's Cave' 94
'First Snow' 104
flava (= *lilioasphodelus*) 19, 28, 29, 43, 52
'Florissant Miss' 86
forrestii 32, 33, **43**, **51**, 59
'Perry's Variety' 43
'Fox Grape' 91, 96
'Frances Fay' 84, 95
'Frank Gladney' 86
'Frans Hals' 92
'French Porcelain' 92
'Frivolous Frills' 105
'Frosted Pink Ice' 87
'Frozen Jade' 77, 97
× *fulcitrina* 23
'Full Reward' 75, 77, 95
fulva 27, 40
   classification 32
   description **44**, 44–6
   growth habit **34**
   history 19, 20, 23, 24
   identification 33
   introduction date 59
   name 28–9
   root characteristics 29
   triploid types 71
   'Chengtu' 44
   'Cypriani' 23, 24, 44–5
   'Europa' 44–5
   'Festival' 45
   'Flore Pleno' 20, 45
   'Hankow' 45
   'Hupehensis' 45

INDEX OF SPECIES, VARIETIES AND HYBRIDS

'Kwanzo' ('Kwanso') 24, 31, 45
'Kwanzo Variegata' 45
'Margaret Perry' 24, 45
'Red Bird' 45–6
'Speciosa' 46
'Theron' 46
  var. *angustifolia* 46–7
  var. *disticha* 20, 23, 40, 47
  var. *littorea* 29, 37, 47, **48**, 52, 59
  var. *longituba* 48, 52
  var. *maculata* 20–1, 23, 48–9, 59
  var. *pauciflora* 49
  var. *rosea* 16, 49, 59
    'Pastel rose' 49
    'Rosalind' 49
  var. *sempervirens* 49–50
'Vieux Carre' 46

'Galena Holiday' 82
'Galena Moon' 77
'Garden Puppet' 87
'Gay Cravat' 92
'Gentle Shepherd' 89
'Georg Rodewald' 110
'George Cunningham' 84
'George Yeld' 24
'Gloria Blanca' 96
'Gold Dust' 24
'Gold Frenzy' 111
'Gold Lace' 26
'Golden Bell' 24
'Golden Chimes' 26, 75, 79, 95, 132
'Golden Prize' 77
'Golden Scroll' 77, 97
'Goldmarie' 111
'Graceful Eye' 90, 97
graminea 20, 23–4, 32, 35, **50**, 51, 59
  f. *humilior* 50
'Green Flutter' 72, 78, 95, 96
'Green Glitter' 77, 95
'Green Puff' 77
'Green Valley' 75, 95
'Grosse Zitrone' 111
'Guardian Angel' 88, 96

hakunensis 32, 35, 51
'Halo' 24
'Hamlet' 97
'Hannover Start' 111

'Happy Returns' 78, 123
'Haymaker' 80
'Heather Green' 86
'Heiteres Rot' 111
'Helle Berlinerin' 111
'Hemlock' 82
'Hesperus' 22, 75, 94
'Hexenritt' 111
'Hi de Ho' 78
'High Noon' 75, 95
'Highland Lord' 96
× *hippeastroides* 23, 51
'Holiday Delight' 92
'Hope Diamond' 90, 95
'Hortensia' 75, 95
'Hudson Valley' 77, 97
'Hyperion' 75

'Ice Carnival' 88, 104
'Ice Castles' 87
'Ida Duke Miles' 77
'Ida Miles' 97
'Imperator' 92
'Irish Elf' 79
'Irongate Glacier' 89
'Irongate Iceberg' 88, 89

'J.S. Gaynor' 24
'James Marsh' 82
'Jane Graham' 26
'Janet Gayle' 83, 86, 95
'Janice Brown' 96, 97
'Jekyll Jewell' 83
'Jenny Wren' 79
'Jerome' 77
'Jest' 95
'Jet Scarlet' 26, 80
'Jim Cooper' 82
'Joan Senior' 88, 89
'Josef Reinermann' 111
'Julia Tanner' 104

'Kaete Waechter' 111
'Kanapaha' 72
'Kathleen Ormerod' 80
'Katrinchen' 100
'Kazuq' 89
'Kevin' 78
'Kindly Light' 75
'King Alfred' 96
'King Haiglar' 82
'King's Cloak' 92, 97
'Kokeshi' 91

'Lady Inara' 87, 138

'Lagerfeuer' 23
'Lavender Flight' 88, 95
'Lavender Mink' 26
'Lemon Bells' 25, 79, 132
'Lemon Mint' 77
'Liberty' 105
'Light The Way' 89
lilioasphodelus **18**, 133
  classification 32
  description 43, 51–2, **52**
  growth habit **46**
  identification 33
  introduction date 59
  name 28–9
  history 15, 16, 19, 22–3, 24
Lilioasphodelus fulva see *fulva*
Lilioasphodelus luteus liliflorus 18
Lilium luteum 18, 19
Lilium non bulbosum 19
'Limited Edition' 77, 128
Liriosphodelus 18
Liriosphodelus phoenicius 18
'Little Brown Koko' 94
'Little Business' 83, 96
'Little Celena' 87, 96
'Little Deeke' 7
'Little Fat Dazzler' 83
'Little Fruit Cup' 93
'Little Grapette' 91, 95, 132
'Little Greenie' 79, 96
'Little Gypsy Vagabond' 93
'Little Infant' 96
'Little Maggie' 93
'Little Melissa' 90
'Little Nicky' 90
'Little Pink Charmer' 87
'Little Rainbow' 61, 96
'Little Red Hen' 83
'Little Showoff' 94
'Little Snowy' 90
'Little Trump' 80
'Little Tyke' 80
'Little Violet Lace' 90
'Little Wart' 90, 96
'Little Woman' 94
'Little Zinger' 83, 96
littorea see *fulva*
'Lona Eaton Miller' 75, 95
longituba see *fulva*
'Look Away' 92
'Lord Camden' 83, 96

INDEX OF SPECIES, VARIETIES AND HYBRIDS

'Love that Pink' 84
'Lula Mae Purnell' 84, 95
'Lullaby Baby' 87, 96
'Luminous Jewel' 89
'Lusty Lealand' 82
lutea 52
× *luteola* 52, **53**
Luteus major 19
Luteus minor 19
'Luxury Lace' 87, 95, 96
'Lynn Hall' 92

'McPick' 75, 79, 96
maculata see *fulva*
'Maikoenigin' 69
'Mallard' 82
'Margaret Marlatt' 82
'Margaret Perry' 24, 45
'Margarite' 26
'Marion Vaughn' 76
'Marsh Pixie' 105
'Martha Adams' 86, 95
'Mary Crocker' 90
'Mary Todd' 78, 95, 97
'Mauna Loa' 78
'May Hall' 84, 95
'Meadow Sprite' 90
'Melon Balls' 84, 96
'Melonencocktail' 111
'Michelle Coe' 84
micrantha 32, 35, 52–3, 55
middendorffii 21, 23–4
 border sites 133
 characteristics 29, 30
 classification 31, 32
 description **53**, 53–4
 growth habit **47**, 70
 identification 34
 introduction date 59
'Midnight Magic' 97
'Mikado' 92
'Ming Porcelain' 86
'Ming Snow' 96
'Mini Skirt' 92
'Mini Stella' 79
'Miniken' 24
minor 20, 23–4, 58, 103
 classification 32, 50
 description 29, **54**
 garden locations 133
 growth habit **51**
 identification 33
 introduction date 59
minor crocea 51
'Missenden' 25

'Moidore' 24
'Moment of Truth' 95, 104
'Mosel' 90
'Mountain Violet' 90
× *mülleri* 23, 54
multiflora 16, 30, 32, 35, **46**, 55, 59
'Multnomah' 85, 95
'My Belle' 86, 95

nana 24
 characteristics 29, 30
 classification 31, 32
 description 55–6, **56**
 growth habit **51**
 identification 33
 introduction date 59
'Naranja' 76, 94
'Natzohm' 111
'Netsuke' 90
'New Series' 97
'Nile Crane' 86
'Nob Hill' 85
'Northbrook Star' 78
'Norton Hall' 25, 82
'Norton Orange' 25, 78, 118
'Norton Tallboy' 25
'Nova' 78

× *ochroleuca* 23, 56
'Olive Bailey Langdon' 90, 95
'Olive Langdon' 96
'Orange Ufo' 111
'Orient' 92
'Oriental Ruby' 81, 95

'Pa Pa Gulino' 86, 96
'Painted Lady' 22, 92, 94
'Pandora's Box' 93, 96
'Panfield Charm' 26, 86
'Panfield Dazzle' 26
'Panfield Plum' 26
'Paper Butterfly' 93, 97
'Pardon Me' 83, 96
'Pat Mercer' 78
'Peach Fairy' 96
'Peach Soufflé' 96
pedicellata 32, 33, 56
'Penelope Vestey' 85
'Pfennigparade' 111
'Phoenician Wealth' 105
'Pink Circle' 86
'Pink Corduroy' 86

'Pink Corsage' 87
'Pink Lightning' 85
'Pink Ufo' 111
'Pioneer' 24
'Playboy' 76, 95
plicata 32, 35, 56, **57**, 59
'Pojo' 79, 96
'Pony' 104
'Potentate' 81, 94
'Prairie Blue Eyes' 90
'Prairie Charmer' 92
'Prester John' 95, 96
'Prima Donna' 85, 94
'Puddin' 79, 96
Puniceus (*Phoenicus*) 19
'Purple Bounty' 105
'Purple Robe' 105
'Pyewacket' 93

'Queen of May' 69
'Quiet Stars' 105
'Quixotic' 104

'Rachel My Love' 96
'Raindrop' 79, 95, 96
'Real Wind' 93
'Red Cup' 81
'Red Mittens' 81, 95
'Red Precious' 26
'Red Roque' 82
'Red Rum' 95, 96
'Regal Air' 81
'Renee' 95, 96
'Reverend Traub' 76
'Revolute' 76, 94
'Rose Emily' 86
'Rosennymphe' 111
'Roter Stammbaum' 111
'Rouqueffeuil' 112
'Royal Heritage' 90, 97
'Royal Reflections' 93
'Ruby Wine' 81
'Rudolf Seyer' 111
'Ruffled Apricot' 86, 95, 97, 118
'Ruffled Pinafore' 85, 94
'Rundblick' 111
'Russian Rhapsody' 90, 95
rutilans 57

'Sabie' 95
'Sail On' 81
'Sally Lake' 104
'Salmon Sheen' 85, 95
'Sammy Russell' 81

INDEX OF SPECIES, VARIETIES AND HYBRIDS

'Sari' 86
'Satin Glass' 88, 95
'Scarlock' 82
'Schoeppinger Anfang' 111
'Schoeppinger Postillon' 111
'Sebastian' 90, 97
sempervirens see *fulva*
'Serene Madonna' 89
serotina (= *thunbergii*) 57, 58
'Shadrach' 104
'Shooting Star' 76
'Shot Silk' 26
'Showamber' 78
'Silkwood' 78
'Siloam' 102
'Siloam Bertie Ferris' 96
'Siloam Bo Peep' 93, 96
'Siloam Button Box' 93
'Siloam Double Classic' 93, 96, 97
'Siloam Double Rose' 93, 96, 97
'Siloam Fairy Tale' 94
'Siloam French Marble' 93
'Siloam Grace Stamile' 96
'Siloam Jim Cooper' 96
'Siloam June Bug' 94, 96
'Siloam Little Girl' 93
'Siloam Mama' 78, 97
'Siloam Pocket Size' 83
'Siloam Purple Plum' 90, 96
'Siloam Red Toy' 83, 96
'Siloam Red Velvet' 82
'Siloam Ribbon Candy' 83
'Siloam Shocker' 93
'Siloam Show Girl' 83
'Siloam Spizz' 97
'Siloam Tee Tiny' 94, 96, 97
'Siloam Uri Winniford' 93, 94
'Siloam Virginia Henson' 96, 97
'Silver Fan' 88, 96
'Silver Ice' 86

'Silver Veil' 86
'Sir Michael Forster' 23
'Ski Chalet' 104
'Skiatook Cardinal' 81, 95
'Smoky Mountain' 86, 97
'Snow Ballerina' 96
'Snow Fairy' 26
'Snowfall' 104
'Snowy Apparition' 96
'So Lovely' 105
'Soft Caress' 96
'Sombrero Way' 97
'Song Sparrow' 79
'Sonnenbarke' 111
'Soudan' 72
'Sovereign' (= 'Beauty') 24
'Spinne in Lachs' 111
'Squeaky' 95
'Stafford' 25, 81
'Stella d'Oro' 69, 79, 95, 96, 123
'Step Forward' 85
'Stern von Rio' 26
'Stroke of Midnight' 96
'Sugar Cookie' 96
sulphurea (= *thunbergii*) 57, 58
'Summer Splendour' 85
'Super Purple' 90, 97
'Suzie Wong' 76, 96
'Swapshop' 93
'Swirling Water' 90, 97

'Tang' 81
'Tender Love' 97
'Tetra Starzynski' 72
'Texan Sunlight' 96
'Thelma Perry' 24, 76
'Thumbelina' 76, 95
thunbergii 21, 23, 24, 38
  classification 32
  description **57**, 57–8
  growth habit **35**
  identification 33
  introduction date 59
'Tinker Bell' 76, 95
'Tiny Pumpkin' 79
'Todd Munroe' 93
'Tonia Gay' 86

'Totnes' 24
'Tovarich' 105
'Toyland' 85, 95
'Tropical Toy' 87

vespertina 39, 58
'Violet Hour' 97
vomerensis 23
× *vomerensis* 58

'Wally Nance' 82
'Waltraud Kroeger' 112
washingtoniana 58, 72
'Water Witch' 91, 132
'Weathermaster' 89
'Westerwaelder Nordlicht' 112
'Whichford' 76
'White Cloud' 88, 96
'White Emeralds' 26, 88
'White Formal' 88, 95
'White Jade' 88
'White Temptation' 89
'White Wings' 104
'Wideyed' 92
'Will Return' 97
'Willard Gardner' 76, 97
'Windsong' 78
'Wine Spoon' 112
'Winnie the Pooh' 87
'Winning Ways' 78, 95
'Winsome Lady' 85, 95
'Wynn' 79
'Wynnson' 96

'Yazoo Soufflé' 96
'Yellow Hammer' 24
'Yellow Lollipop' 96
'Yesterday's Memories' 86, 95
yezoensis 32, 33, 40, 58–9
'Young CHA' 112

'Zarte Wolke' 112
Zephyranthes 40
'Zinfandel' 97
'Zitrone' 23
'Zitronenriese' 112

```
635.93                    c.1-M
ERH      Erhardt, Walter
         Hemerocallis
```

DATE DUE			
MAY 12 2005			

TROY PUBLIC LIBRARY

MAY 16 1996   GAYLORD FR2